CHARIOTS OF FIRE

Adaptation by
Mike Bartlett

Based on the Enigma Productions Limited
Motion Picture
by arrangement with Twentieth Century Fox
Film Corporation
and Allied Stars S.A. Panama
Screenplay by Colin Welland

samuelfrench.co.uk

Copyright © 2011 Chariots of Fire (Stage) U.K. Limited
© 2017 by Mike Bartlett
All Rights Reserved

CHARIOTS OF FIRE is fully protected under the copyright laws of the British Commonwealth, including Canada, the United States of America, and all other countries of the Copyright Union. All rights, including professional and amateur stage productions, recitation, lecturing, public reading, motion picture, radio broadcasting, television and the rights of translation into foreign languages are strictly reserved.

ISBN 978-0-573-11394-9
www.samuelfrench.co.uk
www.samuelfrench.com

FOR AMATEUR PRODUCTION ENQUIRIES

UNITED KINGDOM AND WORLD
EXCLUDING NORTH AMERICA
plays@SamuelFrench-London.co.uk
020 7255 4302/01
UNITED STATES AND CANADA
info@SamuelFrench.com
1-866-598-8449
Each title is subject to availability from Samuel French,
depending upon country of performance.

CAUTION: Professional and amateur producers are hereby warned that *CHARIOTS OF FIRE* is subject to a licensing fee. Publication of this play does not imply availability for performance. Both amateurs and professionals considering a production are strongly advised to apply to the appropriate agent before starting rehearsals, advertising, or booking a theatre. A licensing fee must be paid whether the title is presented for charity or gain and whether or not admission is charged.

The First Class Broadway and West End Professional Rights in this play are controlled by Chariots of Fire (Stage) UK Ltd, 4th Floor Eon House, 138 Piccadilly, London W1J 7NR.

The Professional Rights, excluding First Class Broadway and West End, in this play are controlled by Samuel French Ltd, 24-32 Stephenson Way, London NW1 2HD.

No one shall make any changes in this title for the purpose of production. No part of this book may be reproduced, stored in a retrieval system, or transmitted in any form, by any means, now known or yet to be invented, including mechanical, electronic, photocopying, recording, videotaping, or otherwise, without the prior written permission of the publisher. No one shall upload this title, or part of this title, to any social media websites.

The right of Mike Bartlett to be identified as author of this work has been asserted in accordance with Section 77 of the Copyright, Designs and Patents Act 1988.

THINKING ABOUT PERFORMING A SHOW?

There are thousands of plays and musicals available to perform from Samuel French right now, and applying for a licence is easier and more affordable than you might think

From classic plays to brand new musicals, from monologues to epic dramas, there are shows for everyone.

Plays and musicals are protected by copyright law so if you want to perform them, the first thing you'll need is a licence. This simple process helps support the playwright by ensuring they get paid for their work, and means that you'll have the documents you need to stage the show in public.

Not all our shows are available to perform all the time, so it's important to check and apply for a licence before you start rehearsals or commit to doing the show.

LEARN MORE & FIND THOUSANDS OF SHOWS

Browse our full range of plays and musicals and find out more about how to license a show

www.samuelfrench.co.uk/perform

Talk to the friendly experts in our Licensing team for advice on choosing a show, and help with licensing

plays@samuelfrench.co.uk   020 7387 9373

Acting Editions

BORN TO PERFORM

Playscripts designed from the ground up to work the way you do in rehearsal, performance and study

---

Larger, clearer text for easier reading

Wider margins for notes

Performance features such as character and props lists, sound and lighting cues, and more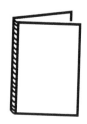

+ CHOOSE A SIZE AND STYLE TO SUIT YOU

STANDARD EDITION

Our regular paperback book at our regular size

SPIRAL-BOUND EDITION

The same size as the Standard Edition, but with a sturdy, easy-to-fold, easy-to-hold spiral-bound spine

LARGE EDITION

A4 size and spiral bound, with larger text and a blank page for notes opposite every page of text. Perfect for technical and directing use

---

LEARN MORE | **samuelfrench.co.uk/actingeditions**

ABOUT THE AUTHOR

Plays for the theatre include: *Wild* (Hampstead Theatre), *Game* (Almeida), *King Charles III* (Almeida Theatre/Wyndham's Theatre/Music Box Theatre, New York), *An Intervention* (Paines Plough/Watford), *Bull* (Sheffield Theatres/Off Broadway/Young Vic), *Medea* (Headlong/Glasgow Citizens/Watford/Warwick), *Chariots of Fire* (Hampstead Theatre/Gielgud Theatre), *13* (National Theatre), *Decade* (co-writer Headlong), *Earthquakes in London* (Headlong/National Theatre), *Love Love Love* (Paines Plough/Plymouth Theatre Royal/Royal Court), *Cock*, *Contractions*, *My Child* (Royal Court Theatre), *Artefacts* (Bush Theatre/Nabokov).

Plays for the radio: *King Charles III*, *Cock*, *Heart*, *The Core*, *Family Man*, *Love Contract* (BBC Radio 4), *The Steps*, *Not Talking* (BBC Radio 3).

As director: *Medea* (Headlong/Glasgow Citizens/Watford/Warwick), *Honest* (Theatre Royal Northampton).

Television includes: *Doctor Foster* (Drama Republic/BBC), *The Town* (Big Talk Productions).

At the 2015 Olivier Awards *King Charles III* won Best New Play and *Bull* won Outstanding Achievement in an Affiliate Theatre. *Love Love Love* won Best New Play in the 2011 Theatre Awards UK and *Cock* won an Olivier Award in 2010 for Outstanding Achievement in an Affiliate Theatre.

MUSIC USE NOTE

Licensees are solely responsible for obtaining formal written permission from copyright owners to use copyrighted music in the performance of this play and are strongly cautioned to do so. If no such permission is obtained by the licensee, then the licensee must use only original music that the licensee owns and controls. Licensees are solely responsible and liable for all music clearances and shall indemnify the copyright owners of the play(s) and their licensing agent, Samuel French, against any costs, expenses, losses and liabilities arising from the use of music by licensees. Please contact the appropriate music licensing authority in your territory for the rights to any incidental music.

USE OF COPYRIGHT MUSIC

A licence issued by Samuel French Ltd to perform this play does not include permission to use the incidental music specified in this copy. Where the place of performance is already licensed by the PERFORMING RIGHT SOCIETY (PRS) a return of the music used must be made to them. If the place of performance is not so licensed then application should be made to the PRS, 2 Pancras Square, London, N1C 4AG (www.mcps-prs-alliance.co.uk).

A separate and additional licence from PHONOGRAPHIC PERFORMANCE LTD, 1 Upper James Street, London W1F 9DE (www.ppluk.com) is needed whenever commercial recordings are used.

IMPORTANT BILLING AND CREDIT REQUIREMENTS

If you have obtained performance rights to this title, please refer to your licensing agreement for important billing and credit requirements.

FIRST PRODUCTION INFORMATION

HUGH HUDSON, BARBARA BROCCOLI, MICHAEL G
WILSON & MICHAEL ROSE
for
CHARIOTS OF FIRE (STAGE) UK LTD
presents

A HAMPSTEAD THEATRE PRODUCTION

FOR COUNTRY
FOR HONOUR
FOREVER

CHARIOTS OF FIRE

ON
STAGE

CHARIOTS OF FIRE
STAGE ADAPTATION BY
MIKE BARTLETT
Based on the Enigma Productions Limited motion picture
By arrangement with Twentieth Century Fox Film
Corporation
And Allied Stars S.A. Panama
Screenplay by Colin Welland

Directed by   EDWARD HALL

Designed by   MIRIAM BUETHER
Costumes by   MICHAEL HOWELLS

Choreographed by   SCOTT AMBLER
Additional music and arrangements by   JASON CARR

Lighting designed by   RICK FISHER
Sound designed by   PAUL GROOTHUIS

Original music by
VANGELIS

CHARACTERS

(IN ORDER OF APPEARANCE)

HAROLD

ERIC

AUBREY

ANDY

REG

JIM

HEAD PORTER

MR RATCLIFFE – his assistant

MASTER OF CAIUS

MASTER OF TRINITY

CHARLIE

FRANK

VARIOUS SOCIETY REPRESENTATIVES

PRESIDENT OF G AND S SOCIETY

SECRETARY OF G AND S SOCIETY

ROBIN

ALASTAIR

COLIN

JENNIE

SANDY

PROVOST

MR LIDDELL

SAM MUSSABINI

JOHN KEDDIE

FRENCH ATHLETE 1

FRENCH ATHLETE 2

JIMMIE

SYBIL

THE ENTIRE CAST OF THE MIKADO

TOFFY

JACKSON SCHOLZ

CHARLIE PADDOCK

FOSTER

REPORTERS

BIRKENHEAD

SUTHERLAND

CADOGAN

THE PRINCE OF WALES

VARIOUS REPORTERS

MANY DIFFERENT RUNNERS

20 COUNTRY'S OLYMPIC TEAMS

FLORENCE

GEORGES ANDRE

THE FRENCH PRESIDENT

TOM WATSON

ANNOUNCER

STAGEHAND

The action of the play is fast, confident and continuous. Always something to focus on, especially in scene changes.

The performance should require effort – an athletic event itself. By the end the performers should be exhausted.

PROLOGUE

As the audience enters, some young contemporary athletes warm up.

They start to run.

We watch them – the effort. The breathing, the sweat.

Somehow the four contemporary athletes become our four runners in 1924.

HAROLD, ERIC, AUBREY *and* **ANDY.**

The whole sequence builds and builds – a celebration of running itself. Amazing, athletic and real.

Then with a swirling and smoke – we're in...

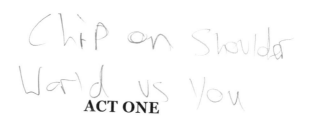

ACT ONE

Part One

Cambridge station 1919. The sound of steam, smoke. In the middle, now in suit and hat, is **HAROLD ABRAHAMS,** *newly arrived at Cambridge. He has a couple of bags, and a pair of running shoes attached by the laces. Porters run back and forth.*

HAROLD Excuse me?

No one stops.

Hey!

Still no one. He turns to the audience.

Dear Mother, my first day at Cambridge was not ideal. For a start, Adolphe's advice concerning porters was, to be short, inaccurate.

A porter goes past carrying bags.

This would not have been a problem had he not also told me to bring so many of my things. I was carrying far more than anyone else.

At which point **AUBREY MONTAGUE** *appears. Upper middle class, shy and carrying even more than* **ABRAHAMS.** *Three bags, books, golf clubs and two tennis racquets.*

Well – almost anyone.

AUBREY *struggles, and in a clownish moment, everything goes everywhere.* HAROLD *looks over and smiles.* AUBREY*'s frustrated.*

AUBREY Dear Papa, the train was full of other first years, talking as if they knew each other already. By the time I got in at the station, I don't mind admitting, I was beginning to feel rather like a spare part.

AUBREY *gathers them up, inefficiently.*

HAROLD Look like you could do with a hand.

AUBREY Oh.

HAROLD My brother Adolphe, he's ten years older than I am, I sought his advice. Get here early, he said, and you'll have someone to carry your bags, see you to college, you won't have to worry about a thing.

AUBREY Ah.

HAROLD But so much for that – do you speak at all old chap?

AUBREY I'm sorry?

HAROLD Do you speak?

AUBREY Oh yes.

HAROLD Good. There you are. All in hand.

AUBREY Montague... Aubrey. I'm a first year.

HAROLD Aren't we all? Come on. Let's make our own way.

AUBREY Right.

HAROLD *finds himself holding...*

HAROLD Two racquets Aubrey?

AUBREY I often break things.

HAROLD I'd never have guessed.

USL

> HAROLD *slings one of* AUBREY'*s bags on his back. From off we hear a porter,* REG.

REG Need a porter sir?

HAROLD Too late I'm afraid, we'll manage on our own.

REG You sure about that sir?

> HAROLD *turns and sees* REG. *He's scarred, with a bandage across his head, and missing an arm. A First World War veteran.*

HAROLD Oh. Well. Thank you. Caius College please.

> *He whistles.* JIM *appears – another veteran, blind, wearing his medals.* REG *loads him up with the bags.*

AUBREY That could've been us. A few months older and the things we'd have seen. Stuck in those trenches.

All Miming

> *Suddenly with the sound of ringing Cambridge bells, the stage is flooded by undergraduates swirling around with bags and books, gowns, hats. The* HEAD PORTER *arrives, with his* ASSISTANT.

HEAD PORTER Gentlemen! Form an orderly queue please gentlemen!

DSL

> *A queue is formed,* HAROLD *and* AUBREY *near the front.*

AUBREY Did he give you any other tips?

HAROLD Who's that?

AUBREY Your brother? Any other advice?

HAROLD Actually yes. He said the most important thing, when one arrives in Cambridge is to make absolutely, doubly sure that no matter what you always—

HEAD PORTER Name!

HAROLD Ah – Abrahams... Harold.

HEAD PORTER Abrahams. Top of the list. Repton is it?

HAROLD That's right. Left a year ago.

HEAD PORTER Been doing your bit have you? France?

HAROLD No. Joined too late.

HEAD PORTER Oh. Bad luck laddie.

HAROLD I beg your pardon?

They look at each other. The **HEAD PORTER** *smiles, patronising, passive aggressive.*

HEAD PORTER Welcome to Caius. Sign here.

He does.

It's across the courtyard, top right hand corner, and up the stairs.

HAROLD Thank you. What are your names?

HEAD PORTER I'm Rogers, head porter – Mr Ratcliffe, my assistant.

HAROLD Well Mr Rogers, Ratcliffe, I ceased to be called laddie when I took up the King's commission. Is that clear?

HEAD PORTER Yes sir. Crystal clear.

HAROLD *goes.* **AUBREY** *steps forward.*

What's your friend studying then?

AUBREY I've no idea.

HEAD PORTER Hmm. Well one thing's certain, with a name like Abrahams, he won't be in the chapel choir, will he?

HAROLD *unpacks his case, and writes a letter, speaking to the audience.*

HAROLD Mother, Adolphe seemed certain it was a terrible idea, but I feel despite everything that's happened, the way he's behaved and all he's done, Father deserves to know that I'm here. All of what I've been given and achieved is in no small part down to—

There's a knock on the door.

And ~~VOICE OFF~~ Shop!

ABRAHAMS *stops writing/unpacking and opens the door. Standing there is* **ANDY**, *Lord Andrew Lindsey, in a very posh suit. Immaculate.*

ANDY Hello. I'm across the corridor. Lord Lindsey. You can call me Andrew, or Lord Lindsey, or Andy, actually. It's up to you.

HAROLD Harold Abrahams.

ANDY Good! Books. Excellent. School?

HAROLD Repton.

ANDY Repton! Marvellous! Eton myself. Hold on... Abrahams. There was a chap, Abrahams, went to Caius, years ago. I read about him. Runner. Broke all kinds of records.

HAROLD My brother.

ANDY Ah! You're the sibling. Smashing.

He pulls a book out from the case.

The Athletic Trainer by Sam Wisdom. Tempted to have a go yourself are you? Yes. Always tricky with famous older brothers isn't it? Probably better off finding your own passions old chap. Don't want to live in the shadow.

Pours Lindsey **HAROLD** Drink, Andrew?

ANDY Very good. Can you believe it Harold?

Cambridge at last. About bloody time.

He smiles, warmly. **HAROLD** *gives him a drink.*

Cheers!

They drink together. There's a knock on the still-open door. It's **AUBREY** – *in his evening suit as well. Similar to* **ANDY**'s *but not nearly as good.*

DSR

AUBREY Oh. Hello.

HAROLD Aubrey! Come in. Drink? This is Lord Lindsey. But we can call him Andrew.

ANDY I'm across the hall. Eton. You?

AUBREY Rugby.

ANDY Oh well. Never mind. Left now, haven't you?

ABRAHAMS *gives* **AUBREY** *his drink.*

AUBREY Thanks.

ANDY Are you getting yourself together then Harold? Ten minutes to freshmans' dinner. You should be changed.

ALL *Men*
ALL PEOPLE THAT ON EARTH DO DWELL
SING TO THE LORD WITH CHEERFUL VOICE
HIM SERVE WITH FEAR, HIS PRAISE FORETELL
COME YE BEFORE HIM AND...

Get dressed
onstage

ABRAHAMS *finishes his letter as he puts on his suit.*

HAROLD Mother. You wouldn't believe it here. It really is another world.

Table
2

The formal dinner is set up.

Ancient buildings.

Choirs more beautiful than you could imagine.

Go
2

A vision. Of England.

Exit CAIUS

GRACE. Sanctificet nobis victum qui cuncta creavit. Amen.
("Let him who hath created all things bless for us what there
is to eat".)

S↓

A shuffling and quietening as **THE MASTER OF CAIUS** *stands. An older man. Dignified.*

CAIUS I take these college war lists and I run down them. Name after name which I cannot read and which we who are older cannot hear without emotion – names which are only names to you, the new college, but which to us summon up face after face, the men they were, the men they might have been. The flower of a generation, of England, cut before their time – they died for England and all that England stands for.

Suddenly we're half way through dinner. The talk is loud and confident.

ANDY Gentlemen. Ambitions! What do you want to be? Charlie?

CHARLIE Doctor all the way. Two brothers and a father already in practice, the family expects.

ANDY Boring. But respectable. Frank?

FRANK Lawyer, I think.

ANDY Yes, you are rather argumentative.

FRANK No I'm not!

ANDY Aubrey?

AUBREY Perhaps, a journalist?

They laugh.

ANDY A journalist? Whatever for?

AUBREY ...Well I like writing.

ANDY Alright then. Journalism for Montague from Rugby. Dear oh dear.

Freeze *The* MASTER *continues. A slow, very different speed to the young men.*

MASTER Now, by tragic necessity, their dreams have become yours. On their behalf let me exhort you, examine yourselves, assess your potential and find where your true chance of greatness lies. For their sakes, for your college and your country, seize this chance, rejoice in it, and let no power nor persuasion deter you in your task.

We're back to the table.

ANDY Harold! Just you left. Ambitions. What will you be?

HAROLD What will I be?

ANDY Yes.

HAROLD *looks straight at him.*

HAROLD Fast.

A moment.

CAIUS Let us pray... ↗ Stand

And we're at the Students' Societies Fair ("Squash").

ALL
THE SOLDIERS OF OUR QUEEN, ALL LINKED IN FRIENDLY TETHER.
UPON THE BATTLE SCENE, THEY FIGHT THE FOE TOGETHER.
THERE EVERY MOTHER'S SON, PREPARED TO FIGHT AND FALL IS.
THE ENEMY OF ONE, THE ENEMY OF ALL IS. THE ENEMY OF ONE,
THE ENEMY OF ALL IS.
THE SOLDIERS OF OUR QUEEN, ALL LINKED IN FRIENDLY TETHER.
UPON THE BATTLE SCENE, THEY FIGHT THE FOE TOGETHER.
THERE EVERY MOTHER'S SON, PREPARED TO FIGHT AND FALL IS.
THE ENEMY OF ONE, THE ENEMY OF ALL IS. THE ENEMY OF ONE,
THE ENEMY OF ALL IS.

The tables from the formal dinner have become stalls for various different societies. People everywhere, noise –
HAROLD *and* **AUBREY** *tour the stalls.*

RUGBY CLUB Spot of rugby?

PRESIDENT Gilbert and Sullivan Society!

FLORA Flora and Fauna! All the green things around you, in jars, in nature, grasses, trees, moss.

HAROLD No thank you.

FLORA *Fungus?*

AUBREY's come over. HAROLD *takes the different cards he's collected.*

HAROLD Aubrey! Rugby Club, Golf Society, Law, Philately – is that all? You're idle man!

Singing begins. AUBREY *turns to face a poster of* SYBIL *Evers, a singer in the D'Oyly Carte.*

ALL

THERE EVERY MOTHER'S SON, PREPARED TO FIGHT AND
   FALL IS.
THE ENEMY OF ONE, THE ENEMY OF ALL IS.
THE ENEMY OF ONE, THE ENEMY OF...

SYBIL, *in the poster, sings a short aria.*

AUBREY Who is she?!

SECRETARY Sybil Evers, bright new star of the D'Oyly Carte.

SYBIL *sings another short aria. A new stall appears, with binoculars and hat, and shouts—*

BIRDWATCHING Birdwatching?

SYBIL *sings another short aria.* AUBREY *continues to look at the poster. The stall is manned by the* SECRETARY *and* PRESIDENT. *They spot* AUBREY *staring.*

SECRETARY Wonderful isn't she?

SYBIL *turns and sings a final short aria – captivating* AUBREY.

AUBREY She's magnificent.

HAROLD What do you think Aubrey? Gilbert and Sullivan?

AUBREY Did a bit at school but—

HAROLD Perfect. Put my friend down.

AUBREY Now wait a minute. I can't sing!

HAROLD Of course you can, and it's a privilege, singing, gifted to the few, and that's the way it should be. Because—

He sings.

"IF EVERYONE IS SOMEBODY...

The others join in with the line from The Gondaliers, except **AUBREY.**

ALL
"THEN NO ONE'S ANYBODY!"

They laugh, **ABRAHAMS** *signs them up as* **AUBREY** *escapes over to the Athletics Club stall. The* **SECRETARY** *is* **ROBIN.**

ROBIN Athletics?

AUBREY Oh rather – four hundred and forty yards mostly.

ROBIN Fill this in with your best times.

He gives him a clipboard. **AUBREY** *starts to fill it in.*

Haven't come across a chap called Abrahams have you?

AUBREY Yes I have, what about him?

ROBIN He's only gone and challenged for the college dash.

AUBREY College dash? What's so special about that?

ABRAHAMS *walks across, wearing an overcoat.*

ROBIN Special? It's special because in seven hundred years of trying, no one's ever done it!

HAROLD *starts to get ready for the dash, as the* **MASTERS** *from* **CAIUS** *and* **TRINITY** *enter, talking, in colonnades outside – daytime.*

TRINITY This Abrahams, what do you know of him?

CAIUS His father's a financier.

TRINITY A financier? What on earth does that mean?

CAIUS I believe it's a euphemism.

TRINITY Ah. Yes.

TRINITY laughs.

Very good.

CAIUS Repton reports academic achievement, of sorts. They also mention he's arrogant, defensive to the point of pugnacity.

TRINITY They invariably are.

AUBREY enters with a scarf which HAROLD flings round, and adopts a swagger.

HAROLD You know Aubrey. I'd never have expected it. But I'm rather confident.

The MASTERS arrive at their vantage point.

TRINITY What about this "attempt". Did they say he can run?

CAIUS Like the wind!

DsR

AUBREY and HAROLD turn the corner, and the stage is flooded with people, CROWDS waving banners, all out in the courtyard to see the (TRINITY) college dash. HAROLD arrives with AUBREY, looking confident and casual. The CROWD cheer. (Cheers for the courage of the man and jeers for his downright affrontery.) The cheering continues as ROBIN tries to get attention.

ROBIN Right. Chaps. Chaps! Excuse me... Oi!

The CROWD fall silent at last – ROBIN drops back into his accent and poise.

Thank you. Let it be known that HM Abrahams of Gonville and Caius has formerly made challenge for the Trinity Court dash!

Cheers.

For those who are not familiar with the rules, they are as follows – the challenger will attempt to run around the perimeter of the court, to and from a fixed point – here – beneath the clock – this clock – within the time taken by the said clock to strike midday. The distance to be covered is traditionally recognised as one of one hundred and eighty-eight paces.

CROWD 2 Do it for Caius!

CROWD 3 Do it for Repton!

STUDENT What have you got on your feet Abrahams? Rockets?

Laughter.

ROBIN We have just a few minutes… Would the challenger ready himself!

> HAROLD *takes off his scarf and overcoat, and starts stretching. The* CROWD *cheer. Meanwhile, above, we see the* MASTERS OF CAIUS *and* TRINITY *watching.*

CAIUS Anyone from Trinity challenging this year?

TRINITY Ah. Well. Here at Trinity, we're rather good at mathematics. So the young chaps decided to measure the court and they discovered the precise reason it has never been achieved.

CAIUS What's that?

TRINITY It simply isn't possible. The dash was conceived as a dream, not a reality. Therefore, having made the calculations, our men decided this year to save their breath. Very enterprising.

Still, Hugh, it's not the achievement that counts is it? The taking part.

> ROBIN *marks a line on the ground using two of the students' hats.*

ROBIN Mr Abrahams. Your position please.

The CROWD *disperses around the theatre, marking the course to be run – we're going through the audience.* HAROLD *goes to the line. A hush descends.*

Owing to the absence of any challenger, Mr Abrahams will run alone.

VOICE Not so!

All heads turn to see ANDY *hurrying through the* CROWD, *his coat over his shoulder, and holding a bottle of champagne. He tosses the champagne to* AUBREY *and the coat to* ROBIN.

ANDY Andrew Lindsey. I race beside my friend. We challenge the Trinity Court in the name of Repton, Eton and Caius!

Cheers. ANDY *turns to* HAROLD.

Chaps told me about it over breakfast, I thought I might push you along a bit.

HAROLD Thanks very much!

They shake hands.

ROBIN Gentlemen! Ten seconds! To your marks, please.

They crouch into position for the marks.

Remember, at the first strike of twelve.

All heads turn to the clock.

ROBIN Five.

CROWD Four.

Three.

Two.

One.

A beat. The CROWD *do an intake of breath and hold it as—*

The bell sounds twelve times. Stillness.

Then on the strike of twelve and **HAROLD** *and* **ANDY** *run. They really run! Around the course – which is the aisles of the theatre. Cheering but no music. Just the sound of voice and scuffle. It's messy and scrabbling and taking into account all the dimensions and obstacles of the design and the theatre. It's real.*

Dong! Dong!

HAROLD *is first down the opening straight. They get to the corner, the* **CROWD** *turn in unison.*

Dong! Dong!

HAROLD *is out of breath – which allows* **ANDY** *to take the lead. Next corner.*

Dong! Dong!

Down the third stretch, neck and neck. Round the corner.

Dong! Dong!

HAROLD *starts to move past* **ANDY** *as they turn the final corner.*

Dong! Dong!

The **CROWD** *all run to line the final stretch and count as the men get to the line.*

CROWD Ten!

Eleven!

HAROLD *flings himself at the line.*

Dong! He's done it! The **CROWD** *cheers!*

ANDY *collapses behind* HAROLD. *The* CROWD *runs to him and he's lifted into the air.* ANDY *gets the champagne from* AUBREY.

AUBREY Well done! Well done Harold!

HAROLD *smiles and they shake hands, hug. Meanwhile up above...*

CAIUS Did they both manage it?

TRINITY Lindsey missed by a whisker.

CAIUS A pity.

TRINITY Still. It's been done. He proved my mathematicians wrong.

Perhaps they are God's people after all.

Surely there can't be a faster man in the kingdom...

He raises his glass and they drink. Below, the champagne is popped.

AUBREY Harold! Wait! I've just realised! You never told me!

HAROLD What's that old man?

AUBREY Your brother's advice. He said to you – do you remember, that day at the start of term – the most important thing!

HAROLD Oh! Well – the most important thing Aubrey...? To win!

They carry HAROLD *off, as above... They begin to sing* **"TO BE AN ENGLISHMAN"** *as they leave...*

STUDENT. HE IS AN ENGLISHMAN...

ALL BUT IN SPITE OF ALL TEMPTATIONS, TO BELONG TO OTHER NATIONS,

HE REMAINS AN ENGLISHMAN, HE REMAINS AN ENGLISH...

Which mixes with...

Part Two

A highland gathering – 1920.

*Two Scottish boys, **ALASTAIR** and **COLIN**, enter. They're about sixteen, working class, in shorts and caps – it all feels very different to what we've seen so far.*

*A woman (**JENNIE**) enters and puts up some bunting. The boys watch her.*

ALASTAIR Go on.

COLIN No.

Pause.

ALASTAIR She's looking.

COLIN Will you leave it alone? I'm busy.

ALASTAIR Oh, with what? You're taking it all so seriously. It's just a run. What are you up to?

COLIN Warming myself.

ALASTAIR I'm sure she could help you out with that...

COLIN Shut your mouth. I mean for the race. He'll be watching.

Beat.

ALASTAIR *(to JENNIE)* Excuse me? Are you Eric Liddell's sister?

JENNIE Oh – yes.

ALASTAIR What's your name?

Beat.

JENNIE Jennie.

ALASTAIR Me and my friend here, we've come to see Mr Liddell.

JENNIE Yes. We're all pleased he's come. My parents are back from the mission in China, so it'll be good to be together.

And on a gathering day. We'll have a nice time. I hope you boys do too.

She smiles and goes back to the bunting.

ALASTAIR My friend Colin, he's got a question for you.

COLIN What? No I haven't.

ALASTAIR She won't bite, will you Miss Liddell?

JENNIE I should be getting back—

ALASTAIR *(shoving* **COLIN***)* Go on!

COLIN I just wondered if you might like to have a...cup of tea?

JENNIE How old are you?

COLIN Nearly sixteen.

JENNIE You boys should show some respect.

ALASTAIR I don't think that was the answer he was after.

ERIC LIDDELL *enters. Calm, but strong. Wearing a tweed suit.*

ERIC Everything alright there?

JENNIE No it's not.

COLIN *is wide eyed.* **ALASTAIR** *annoyed.*

ALASTAIR Nice suit mister!

COLIN Alastair—

ALASTAIR We're just helping this lady with the decoration, there's no bother—

COLIN Alastair—

ALASTAIR Why don't you go off back where you came from? Mind your own business?!

He laughs, cheeky.

JENNIE Eric...

ERIC Jennie. Are you alright?

ALASTAIR ...Eric?

COLIN Eric.

ALASTAIR Oh. Eric? Oh no!

ERIC *looks at the boys.*

ERIC You boys taking part in the race this afternoon?

COLIN Aye. That is – yes sir. We are.

ERIC Maybe you should go and practise then.

ALASTAIR Aye. Good to meet you Mr Liddell. Come on Colin. Stop messing about.

COLIN *stares at* ERIC *for a moment, then* ALASTAIR *grabs him and they run off.*

JENNIE Those boys knew I was your sister. They've doubled the crowd for the gathering this year, just because of the guest of honour.

ERIC I can't help it if they ask me to present a few prizes, say a few words.

JENNIE About sport.

ERIC Aye. It's what I'm known for. What else would I...

He looks at her – can see there's a distance between them.

Are you pleased to see me Jennie?

JENNIE When was the last time you spoke about God Eric? I don't know when I last heard you mention him. Perhaps later on you should—

ERIC *looks at her. The sound of bagpipes from off.*

...what's that noise?

SANDY enters, ERIC's best friend. He's got bagpipes strapped round him. He plays them as he comes in. He's not great but he can get a tune out. It's a strange moment. ERIC smiles. JENNIE looks at him.

He finishes. Out of breath. He smiles. Warm.

SANDY   Got them in Edinburgh. Knew I was coming back with Eric here, thought it might lend a certain charm to proceedings. Been practising. What do you think?

ERIC   You're terrible Sandy.

SANDY   You see Jennie – say what you like about Eric, at least he's honest.

JENNIE   What I say? No one cares what I have to say about him. It's all in the papers these days.

SANDY   Well, he's got a special talent.

JENNIE   We've known that since he was a boy, Sandy, and it's nothing to do with running.

SANDY   They're asking for you Eric. They want you to start the under twelves off.

I'll join you in a minute. Here's the pistol.

He gives it to ERIC.

Mind you don't shoot the children.

ERIC   I'll do my best.

He looks at JENNIE.

It's good to come home Jennie. It's good to see you.

He goes off to a CROWD who look out at the under twelves race. He speaks to them, and prepares to start the race. SANDY and JENNIE look at each other.

JENNIE   You don't think he's got enough on, with the rugby? Now you want him to race?

SANDY Jennie, you've seen him on the field, with the ball in his hands, just imagine—

JENNIE Don't spoil him Sandy. He's a good man.

SANDY It's not me. He'll do what he must.

    ERIC *with the* **CROWD**. *The pistol in the air.*

ERIC On your marks.

    JENNIE *and* **SANDY** *look at each other.*

SANDY We're grown up now. On our own paths. We've got to—

JENNIE Oh! I can't have a conversation with you!

SANDY Why not?

JENNIE That thing! You look ridiculous!

    ERIC *with the pistol...*

ERIC Set...

SANDY Do you want me to play another tune for you?

JENNIE No I don't. I want you to—

SANDY No - wait a minute, if I just—

JENNIE Sandy - please!

> **ERIC** *fires the pistol. The race begins.* **SANDY** *starts playing,* **JENNIE** *smiles, despite herself and a* **CROWD** *of boys, girls, men and women come on, some in dancing clothes, others in kilts, running kit, holding tables, flowers, bunting.*
>
> *The scene becomes the award ceremony at the end of the day.* **ERIC** *gives a silver cup to the winner of the under twelves race. The boy is beaming. Then* **ERIC** *turns and starts to give a speech. The others sit at trestle tables around him -* **SANDY, JENNIE, ERIC**'*s mother and father, other family members, and the* **PROVOST**, *in charge of proceedings.*

ERIC   You know, ladies and gentlemen. One of the real compensations of achieving a certain notoriety is that occasionally, you're asked to come along and give things away. It's often said that giving beats receiving, and let me tell you that the look of delight of those little boys' faces was worth ten of any of the tin pots I've got gathering dust on my Edinburgh sideboard.

When we were in China, my father here, he's always waxing lyrical about his wee home in the glen, but being born across there, like my brothers and sisters, I suffered from a natural incredulity. But looking about me now, at the heather and the hills, feeling the air, and listening to the music of all your voices, I can see he was right. It's very special.

Thank you for welcoming us home, those years ago. Thank you for welcoming me back today. And for reminding me that I am and will be whilst I breathe – a Scot.

Clapping from the CROWD. *The* PROVOST *stands. As the clapping dies,* SANDY *gets up.*

SANDY   Excuse me Mr Provost sir. Before you allow Eric here to go, is it not true that the main event of the meeting is yet to be run?

PROVOST   It is. The four hundred and forty yards.

SANDY   Well, do you not think, if we can find some kit, we might persuade Scotland's finest wing to show us his paces?

The CROWD *approve.* JENNIE *does not.*

What say you Eric?

Almost to JENNIE.

Show us what you can do?

To applause ERIC *changes, takes off his jacket and lines up with the other runners, which includes* ALASTAIR *and* COLIN.

PROVOST Clear the track! On your marks... Set... Go!

The **PROVOST** *sounds the pistol.*

The race is run on a traditional revolve, with the **CROWD** *round the outside.* **ERIC** *is out in front quickly. He's wiping the floor with them.*

In the last straight, his head goes back, the arms start windmilling – something we'll see every time he runs.

The tape is out...and he crashes through it.

The **CROWD** *cheers! Gathers round to congratulate him. Especially* **SANDY**.

SANDY You see Eric?! Didn't I tell you?

JENNIE speaks almost to herself as the scene changes. Psalms 119:9-16. The sound of a church bell – maybe a hymn in the distance.

JENNIE Wherewithal shall a young man cleanse his way? By taking heed thereto according to thy word.

SANDY turns to ERIC's father.

SANDY Surely a touch of liberality would do no harm?

By the time the music finishes, it's the family home, just after Sunday lunch. There's **ERIC**'s *father,* **JENNIE**, *and* **SANDY** *– a visitor.*

MR LIDDELL Sandy the kingdom of God isn't a democracy. There's no discussion, no deliberation as to what road to take. One right. One wrong, one absolute ruler.

SANDY A dictator, you mean?

JENNIE No!

MR LIDDELL Aye, but a benign, loving dictator.

SANDY So much for your freedom of choice.

JENNIE Oh! Will he stop?

ERIC You've still got a choice Sandy. No one's forcing you to follow him.

SANDY *looks at him.*

SANDY Reverend Liddell, might I be permitted to speak?

JENNIE First time you've asked permission—

SANDY Through Eric here, I've come to know you, and your family, very well. You've welcomed me, and been most accommodating over the years, of my...eccentricities – now you, along with Mrs L and young Ernest, are leaving. I want to wish you bon voyage and safe journey back to China, and may the years ahead be happy and content. For those who remain...

He looks at ERIC *and* JENNIE.

...may God protect them, inspire them, and lead them to glory.

JENNIE Thank you Sandy.

MR LIDDELL You talk of glory. Well, I know what you're referring to, Eric. We're proud of you. You're a lucky young man, you possess many gifts. As we saw yesterday.

He looks straight at him.

How good are you Eric?

ERIC Well I...

SANDY You saw him Mr Liddell. He'll run for Scotland before the month's out.

MR LIDDELL Really?

SANDY And after that, the sky's the limit—

ERIC No—

SANDY Maybe, one day, the Olympics.

MR LIDDELL The Olympic Games?

He's impressed.

JENNIE You know where this leads. Father, I can see it. It's all he thinks about. We're losing him.

MR LIDDELL Is that right Eric? Are you lost? Do you know what matters?

A moment. **ERIC** *looks at his father.*

COLIN *(offstage)* Alastair! No!

Suddenly a football smashes through the window and lands on the table. There's shouting from off. Everyone stands, but it's **ERIC** *who picks up the ball, strides over, opens the door, to find...* **COLIN**.

Ohhhh! I'm sorry sir – the others ran away. We didn't mean to – we'll pay, somehow we'll—

ERIC What's your name?

COLIN Colin sir.

ERIC What are you doing?

COLIN Football sir.

ERIC You know what day it is?

COLIN Aye.

ERIC Tell me then.

COLIN Sunday.

ERIC The Sabbath's not a day for football, is it?

Beat.

COLIN No.

ERIC *looks at him, cowering, mortified.*

I'm sorry. I...

He gives up – utterly humiliated, crushed. His life's dreams abandoned.

Oh.

He turns to go.

ERIC Are you up early in the morning?

COLIN Me...me ma gets me up at seven.

ERIC We'll have a game then...okay?

COLIN You and me, Mr Liddell?

ERIC Aye, and anyone else. Tell your friends. I'll give you a five goals start.

COLIN Oh! Thanks! *(As he goes)* Alastair! You'll never guess what...!

> **COLIN** *smiles and runs off.* **JENNIE** *begins to sweep up the glass.*

JENNIE Eric you've got a train to catch at nine o'clock!

ERIC Plenty of time. Do you want him growing up thinking God's a spoilsport?

> **MR LIDDELL** *has been watching all this with amusement and pride.*

MR LIDDELL You're the proud possessor of many gifts Eric—

ERIC I know, I'm lucky, but they're not—

MR LIDDELL —and as I see things, it's your sacred duty to put them to good use.

Run like we know you can, strong and true, and the mission can only gain from your success.

JENNIE But...Pa you've always said—

MR LIDDELL Jennie you can praise the Lord by peeling a potato if you peel it to perfection. And, you'll be here. To keep him on the straight and narrow. Won't you?

JENNIE *looks at them, slightly betrayed.*

JENNIE ...I should take these.

She goes with the teacups.

MR LIDDELL For years now, even when you were a boy, we've said we needed a muscular Christian to make folk sit up and listen. Well... Maybe we've found him. Under our roof. Don't compromise Eric.

Run in God's name. And let the world stand back in wonder.

They stand and leave. ERIC *stays on stage, puts on a coat, takes out a Bible, and starts to speak – preaching, growing in confidence throughout.*

ERIC I want to compare faith to running in a race. It's hard, requires concentration of will, energy of soul. You experience elation when breaking the tape, especially if you've got a bet on it.

But how long does that elation last? You go home, maybe your dinner's burnt, maybe you haven't got a job. So who am I to say "believe", "have faith" in the face of life's realities.

HAROLD *enters, running round and round, training, harder and harder...*

I would like to give you something more permanent, but I can only point the way. I'm afraid I have no formula for winning the race. Everyone runs in her own way or his own way.

The sound of a hymn being sung.

Then where does the power come from to see the race to its end? From within... If you commit yourself to the love of Christ then that is how you run the straight race.

ERIC *leaves.* HAROLD *comes to rest.*

Part Three

Rest- *DSR* (handwritten annotation in left margin)

HAROLD *stands exhausted. In the distance we can hear a hymn being sung in an echo-ey church – louder now.*

HAROLD *stands for a moment, catches his breath. A couple of other very English and posh undergrads walk past, looking down on him.* HAROLD *spots them.*

UNDERGRADS
ALL CREATURES OF OUR GOD AND KING, LIFT UP YOUR VOICE AND WITH US SING, ALLELUIA! ALLELUIA!

They leave.

Then HAROLD *has an idea – and begins to chant...*

HAROLD Barukh ata Adonai Eloheinu Melekh ha-olam, asher kid'shanu b'mitzvotav v'tzivanu l'hadlik ner shel Shabbat.

AUBREY What was that?

He turns – hadn't noticed AUBREY *watching.*

HAROLD A blessing for the candles, before the Sabbath.

AUBREY I didn't realize you knew Hebrew.

HAROLD My mother said it, every week, when I was a child. I don't spend much time on it now. But stood here, I realised I'd be the first person to ever say that prayer ~~in this room~~. *here*

AUBREY *smiles – confused, but wants to understand.*

AUBREY Out running again?

HAROLD Yes Aubrey. Running again.

AUBREY You go every day. You're exhausted. Have a day off at least. We're going into the country tomorrow. Andy's got a car. You should come.

HAROLD *doesn't reply, thinking.*

AUBREY Does it really bother you?

HAROLD What?

AUBREY Being Jewish... When people talk about it.

HAROLD They don't. That's the problem. Sometimes I say to myself, Harold, you're imagining all this, and then I see the look again, or catch it on the edge of a remark – a cold reluctance in a handshake. You won't understand Aubrey, but I sense it all the time.

A don walks past.

My father was a stall-holder. When he arrived here, a Lithuanian Jew, he barely spoke a word of English, but he loved this country, the people, the landscape and he worked hard, every day, to make true gentlemen of his sons...

But the old man forgot one thing. He never realised that this England of his is Christian and Anglo Saxon and so is every brick of the universities, courts, every corridor of power. And those who stalk them, guard them – with jealousy and venom. Not just Cambridge, not just London, but across the country.

AUBREY So what can you do? Grin and bear it?

HAROLD No Aubrey. I'm going to practise and study and train, every hour of the day.

HAROLD *pulls himself together, he's going to keep going, round the block again.*

AUBREY You don't want to come with us tomorrow then?

HAROLD No, I'm going to Scotland tomorrow.

AUBREY What? Scotland? Why on earth would you go to *Scotland?*

HAROLD I have to know what I'm up against Aubrey. Because I'm going to take them on. All of them. And run them off their feet!

A crack of thunder. **HAROLD** *runs off. A man walks past with a large sign, which makes it clear – we're at the Scottish Athletic Association games: Scotland V France – 2nd June, 1923.*

ERIC *enters with* **SANDY.**

SANDY Picked a day for it didn't they? Still, gives the Frogs a taste of Scotland. And us an advantage – we're used to it.

ERIC You missed me speaking Sandy—

SANDY Sorry Eric, but I had a meeting—

ERIC Some of the French came along. Probably couldn't understand my accent, but they listened anyway. What meeting?

SANDY I was speaking to a colleague.

ERIC Who's that?

SANDY A trainer.

ERIC Who?

VOICE No. Mr Mcgrath, not a trainer.

SAM MUSSABINI *enters, in his straw hat and moustache. No umbrella.*

SAM I'm a coach. This him then? Mr Liddell. Pleased to meet you at last. Mussabini.

ERIC Sam Mussabini?

SAM That's it. Tell me. How do you rate your chances?

ERIC Fair.

SAM I'd not argue with that. But you keep on surprising us, don't you lad? So who knows?

JOHN KEDDIE *appears.*

KEDDIE Er! Excuse me! Excuse me!

SAM Oh. Here's trouble.

SANDY Come on Eric. Let's go inside. There's an hour before the race.

ERIC Good to meet you.

SAM You too Mr Liddell.

They go, as KEDDIE *gets to them.*

KEDDIE Mr Mussabini?

SAM That's correct.

KEDDIE I'm not sure if you will know who I am? My name is Keddie. Colonel John Keddie, I'm—

SAM President of the Scottish three As, yes I know, and I'm glad to know you sir.

KEDDIE Ah. Well. I see.

Two FRENCH ATHLETES *jog past.*

FRENCH 1 Bonjour, Mr Sam!

SAM Bonjour!

FRENCH 2 Bonjour.

SAM How's the leg? Nasty fall back there.

FRENCH 1 Ah! Is not hurt, I think.

KEDDIE Mr Mussabini—

SAM Good luck!

FRENCH 1 Merci!

FRENCH 2 Merci.

They jog on.

KEDDIE Mr Mussabini if I may interrupt—

SAM Sam.

KEDDIE Well – yes, you're very welcome of course, and we're all aware of your reputation.

SAM Well thank you—

KEDDIE But I felt it necessary to remind you that we do have a strict amateur code. This is not the place for a *professional* coach, such as yourself. Our boys are here for the love of sport, nothing else.

SAM Don't you worry. I'm here spectating, that's all.

KEDDIE Ah. Well. Alright. That's very good to know. Thank you. I...um. I hope you enjoy the games.

He walks away, head held high – job done.

SAM Games? You must be joking. I've seen better organised riots.

HAROLD *enters, looking around.* **SAM** *watches him for a moment, before putting him out of his misery.*

You alright lad?

HAROLD Stand B?

SAM Over there.

They recognise each other. A moment.

HAROLD Right. Thanks. Thank you.

A bell rings. **HAROLD** *moves on.* **SAM** *looks as he goes. Drags on his cigarette. The six athletes enter,* **HAROLD** *takes up his position to watch, as does* **SAM**. *The athletes, three Scottish, including* **ERIC**, *and three French, stand near the starting line.*

KEDDIE *holds the pistol.*

KEDDIE Gentlemen to your marks. Four hundred and forty yards.

They take up their positions.

VOICE Come on Scotland!

VOICE Vive la France!

KEDDIE Get set... Go!

They all stand up straight, rather than crouching...

The pistol fires. The **CROWD** *cheers – and the* **ATHLETES** *...count...*

The six men count the numbers of the distance as fast as they can, while standing on the spot.

ATHLETES One, two, three, four, five—

(in French) Six, seven, eight, nine, ten—

(in English) Eleven, twelve, thirteen, fourteen, fifteen, twenty, twenty-five—

(in French) Thirty, thirty-five, forty—

(in English) Forty-five, fifty—

They keep going, tense, competitive, jostling between them—

(in English) Sixty, seventy, eighty—

(in French) Ninety, one hundred, one-hundred-and-ten, one-hundred-and-twenty, one-hundred-and-thirty—

(in English) One-hundred-and-forty, one-hundred-and-fifty, one-hundred-and-sixty, one-hundred-and-seventy, one-hundred-and-eighty—

(in French) One-hundred-and-ninety, two hundred—

The **FRENCH ATHLETE** *next to* **ERIC** *pushes him, he trips and falls, the others continue counting.*

(in English) Two-hundred-and-ten, two-hundred-and-twenty, two-hundred-and-thirty, two-hundred-and-forty, two-hundred-and-fifty, two-hundred-and-sixty—

SAM Get up lad!

ERIC *stands back up and keeps going but he's behind—*

ERIC   Two-hundred-and-ten, two-hundred-and-twenty, two-hundred-and-thirty, two-hundred-and-forty—

OTHERS   Two hundred-and-seventy, two hundred-and-eighty,   two   hundred-and-ninety,   three   hundred, three-hundred-and-ten—

They keep going. ERIC *now determined.* SANDY *is with his friend* JIMMIE.

JIMMIE He'll never do it.

SANDY Oh don't you believe it. His head's not back yet.

ERIC   Two hundred-and-seventy, two hundred-and-eighty,   two   hundred-and-ninety,   three   hundred, three-hundred-and-ten—

OTHERS   Three-hundred-and-twenty, three-hundred-and-thirty, three-hundred-and-forty, three-hundred-and-fifty, three-hundred-and-sixty—

ERIC Three-hundred-and-twenty, three-hundred-and-thirty, three-hundred-and-forty—

OTHERS Three-hundred-and-seventy, three-hundred-and-eighty, three-hundred-and-ninety—

SANDY Come on.

ERIC *flings his head back and shouts.*

ERIC   Three-hundred-and-fifty, three-hundred-and-sixty, three-hundred-and-eighty, four hundred—

ALL *(together)* Four-hundred-and-ten, four-hundred-and-twenty, four-hundred-and-thirty—

ERIC Four-hundred-and-forty!

With that he collapses over the line, the others finish but are not as exhausted.

SANDY *and* JIMMIE *rush to* ERIC. SAM *comes over too, as soon as he can. We notice* HAROLD, *watching it all from a distance... The* CROWD *gathers round.*

SANDY Well done Eric!

SAM Get back, get back, give him air, give him *air.*

SANDY *and* SAM *crouch by* ERIC.

SANDY He'll be alright. Get his clothes!

JIMMIE *runs off.*

SAM You take good care of him Mr Mcgrath, because if you drop him you'll never find another like him. It was not the prettiest quarter I've ever seen Mr Liddell, but it certainly was the bravest.

With SANDY's *support, he stands. The* CROWD *applauds and he's taken away.* SAM *watches.*

SANDY Thank you.

They go, as does the CROWD, *to reveal* HAROLD, *still standing there.*

From Rostra

HAROLD Wisdom.

SAM What? ← Jump down,

HAROLD Sam Wisdom. X - Sam

SAM No.

HAROLD Yes I've got your book. There's a frontispiece with your photograph.

SAM I'm not Sam Wisdom.

HAROLD I'll get the bloody book and prove it if you like—

SAM Not any more. I took Wisdom for the wrong reasons. Sam Mussabini. That's what I'm called these days son—

HAROLD You're Sam Mussabini?

SAM I am.

HAROLD The trainer.

SAM The coach.

HAROLD Walker, Applegarth – they broke the records – because of you.

SAM You flatter me Mr Abrahams.

HAROLD Sam Wisdom is Sam Mussabini.

SAM I hope you're quicker on the track than you are in this conversation. Harold.

HAROLD Oh. Well. Oh. Harold? You know who I am.

SAM Seen your photograph too.

HAROLD Oh.

SAM Cambridge boy. I hear you're driven to win.

HAROLD I'm fast.

SAM Faster than him?

He's talking about **ERIC**.

HAROLD That's why I'm here. I'd heard he was the best but I've never seen such drive, such commitment in a runner. He unnerves me.

SAM So he should. I doubt there's better in the country this minute. You should practice Mr Abrahams. Looks like you've got competition.

He turns to go.

HAROLD Mr Mussabini. Help me.

SAM I beg your pardon?

HAROLD If you can do for me what you did for the others! For Walker, and Applegarth. I'll work, I'll work hard but I need discipline, I need you. Please. I can run fast, but I think I can run even faster. I want an Olympic medal. It's waiting for me, but I can't get it on my own!

SAM *looks at him.*

SAM Tell me Mr Abrahams. Are you married?

HAROLD No.

SAM Well when the right girl comes along, how would you feel if she popped the question?

HAROLD Well I'd... I'd...oh...

HAROLD *looks – realises – he's messed this up.*

SAM It's the coach that does the asking.

He laughs a little.

Lads like you. Come and go.

But Liddell?

You can't put in what God's left out. His technique's a disaster, head back, arms like windmills, but you saw him.

You'll do your best I'm sure, but why do you run lad, eh?

What for? You don't really know.

He does. That's the difference.

You've got an engine Mr Abrahams I'm sure. But there's no fuel. No *life*. You need to live a little.

And anyway, I'm too busy. Goodbye.

He leaves HAROLD *standing on his own.*

HAROLD Life?

*One singer (*SYBIL*) enters – from The Mikado.*

[handwritten: Catch eyes]

GIRL LIFE IS A JOKE THAT'S JUST BEGUN.

> **HAROLD** *looks at her – a connection. A moment between them. Two other* **GIRL SINGERS** *enter – from The Mikado.*

SINGERS

> THREE LITTLE MAIDS FROM SCHOOL ARE WE
> PERT AS A SCHOOL-GIRL WELL CAN BE
> FILLED TO THE BRIM WITH GIRLISH GLEE
> THREE LITTLE MAIDS FROM SCHOOL.

> *As* **HAROLD** *changes, and* **AUBREY** *watches, a full D'Oyly Carte production of this scene from The Mikado enters. Costumes, lights, this is a professional thing.*

SINGERS

> EVERYTHING IS A SOURCE OF FUN.

AUBREY There! Look!

[handwritten: DYR]

HAROLD I am Aubrey. I *am...*

AUBREY At the end.

SINGERS

> NOBODY'S SAFE, FOR WE CARE FOR NONE
> LIFE IS A JOKE THAT'S JUST BEGUN
> THREE LITTLE MAIDS FROM SCHOOL.

> *As the women sing,* **HAROLD** *is joined at the side of the stage, watching, by* **AUBREY**, **ANDY**, *the* **PRESIDENT** *and the* **SECRETARY**. *They have opera glasses etc.*

> THREE LITTLE MAIDS WHO, ALL UNWARY
> COME FROM A LADIES' SEMINARY
> FREED FROM ITS GENIUS TUTELARY
> THREE LITTLE MAIDS FROM SCHOOL,
> THREE LITTLE MAIDS FROM SCHOOL.

> **AUBREY**'s *captivated.*

AUBREY Sybil Evers. The voice of a heavenly angel, those eyes, the most beautiful, kindest features in the world, I haven't spoken to her yet but I'm sure that when I do, she'll turn out to be absolutely charming – oh Harold I've never seen any girl like it!

He looks round. **HAROLD**'s *gone.*

Harold?

SINGERS
ONE LITTLE MAID IS A BRIDE, YUM-YUM
TWO LITTLE MAIDS IN ATTENDANCE COME
THREE LITTLE MAIDS IS THE TOTAL SUM
THREE LITTLE MAIDS FROM SCHOOL
FROM THREE LITTLE MAIDS TAKE ONE AWAY
TWO LITTLE MAIDS REMAIN, AND THEY
WON'T HAVE TO WAIT VERY LONG, THEY SAY
THREE LITTLE MAIDS FROM SCHOOL, THREE LITTLE MAIDS
    FROM SCHOOL
THREE LITTLE MAIDS WHO, ALL UNWARY
COME FROM A LADIES' SEMINARY
FREED FROM ITS GENIUS TUTELARY
THREE LITTLE MAIDS FROM SCHOOL, THREE LITTLE MAIDS
    FROM SCHOOL.

The song ends. All applaud.

AUBREY What do you think?

PRESIDENT Not bad, but I'd hardly call it professional—

AUBREY I meant the girl. Sybil Evers!

ANDY Harold's gone topsy for her.

AUBREY Harold? I've been after her for ages, he's only just set eyes on her!

ANDY Do him good. First time I've seen him interested in anything that isn't running.

AUBREY Where is he anyway?

PRESIDENT I think he's gone backstage.

AUBREY In the *interval?!* Why?

ANDY Why do you think?

AUBREY That's simply *not on*, you hear me? The *interval...?*

HAROLD *appears in evening gear.*

HAROLD Dinner! All set. Tonight. Turns out her kid brother loves athletics, can't get enough of me. Cheers. What *is* the matter Aubrey?

Waiters enter humming.

AUBREY I think I'm going to be sick.

> **HAROLD** *laughs and downs his champagne. The production re-enters singing "THE FLOWERS THAT BLOOM IN THE SPRING", as the table is set for* **HAROLD** *and* **SYBIL**. *They meet and he kisses her hand.*

HAROLD

THE FLOWERS THAT BLOOM IN THE SPRING

AUBREY

TRA LA

ALL

BREATHE PROMISE OF MERRY SUNSHINE—
AS WE MERRILY DANCE AND WE SING, TRA LA,
WE WELCOME THE HOPE THAT THEY BRING, TRA LA,
OF A SUMMER OF ROSES AND WINE, OF A SUMMER OF ROSES
    AND WINE.

SYBIL *is given a royal welcome – applause – her coat taken and the chair made ready. An old man approaches and seems to know her – they kiss, and then he goes.* `1

AND THAT'S WHAT WE MEAN WHEN WE SAY THAT A THING
IS WELCOME AS FLOWERS THAT BLOOM IN THE SPRING.
TRA LA LA LA LA, TRA LA LA LA LA
TRA LA
TRA LA LA LA LA, TRA LA LA LA LA, TRA LA LA LA LA.

CRITIC An exquisite Yum-Yum, my dear.

ALL

> TRA LA LA LA LA LA.

> SYBIL *and* HAROLD *sit.*

HAROLD Who was that man?

SYBIL Oh. A critic. You have to kiss them. Part of the job I'm afraid.

HAROLD Well he obviously enjoyed it. The look on his face.

SYBIL He enjoyed the kiss, but as for the show, it's always smiles on the night – the poison comes in the morning.

HAROLD Well I thought you were wonderful.

SYBIL A bit off, I thought. I don't know if you noticed but one of our little maids has gone and got herself preggers with a gondolier. We had to send on her second so the trio wobbled more than the scenery. Disaster.

> *The waiter,* TOFFY, *arrives with cocktails.*

Thank you Toffy, this is Mr Abrahams, he's very fast and very famous, perhaps you've read about him in the papers?

TOFFY Of course, it's a pleasure to meet you Mr Abrahams.

SYBIL He's trying the special for the first time tonight. The special's a kind of cocktail de maison, devised by Toffy himself. Go on Harold, give it a whirl.

> HAROLD *drinks.*

HAROLD Excellent.

SYBIL There Toffy. A friend for life. My favourite please.

TOFFY Of course madam, and for you sir?

> HAROLD *looks at the menu, then closes it.*

HAROLD The same!

TOFFY Excellent. Thank you sir.

He takes the menu then goes.

HAROLD What have I let myself in for?

SYBIL Wait and see. I love a surprise. Like you tonight. Here I am sitting with the famous Harold Abrahams. I tell you, my brother won't half be jealous.

HAROLD Mine too.

A beat.

SYBIL Are you ruthless?

HAROLD I beg your pardon?

SYBIL Timothy says you're ruthless.

HAROLD Timothy...

SYBIL My brother. He says that's the reason you win. Competition with that other one – what's his name? Eric Liddell.

HAROLD I don't look back if that's what he means.

SYBIL Why running Harold?

Well?

HAROLD Why singing?

SYBIL I *love it*. Always have. When one sings nothing gets better or worse, in the world. In that moment, it's all that matters. Oh, I sound dreadfully romantic don't I?

HAROLD Not at all. *Sexay*

SYBIL So? Why running?

Beat.

HAROLD It's the same. I love it too.

SYBIL Timothy said ruthless. It's more than love.

HAROLD What do you think then?

She looks at him.

SYBIL I think you're an addict.

HAROLD ...

SYBIL It's a compulsion. I suspect, for you, Harold Abrahams, running is a weapon. You've got something to prove.

HAROLD How could you possibly know that?

SYBIL There's something in your eyes. It's not like other men.

There's something burning in there.

Beat.

HAROLD I suppose you might be right. Perhaps a weapon. Yes.

SYBIL A weapon against what?

HAROLD Being Jewish I suppose.

SYBIL Whatever do you mean? You're not serious?

HAROLD Yes.

SYBIL What difference does that make?

HAROLD You're not Jewish, or you wouldn't ask.

Beat.

SYBIL Nothing's going to stop you. Is it?

He looks at her, takes her hand. He's found something he was looking for.

HAROLD No.

SYBIL *loves the intensity. She's fascinated.*

SYBIL Jewish.

You're a funny old stick Harold Abrahams.

Life isn't that bad is it?

They look at each other.

Then **TOFFY** *arrives with the dishes.*

TOFFY Les pieds de porc anglais, madam. Pigs' Trotters sir.

SYBIL *gasps.* **HAROLD** *looks at her. Then they both laugh.*

ALL
> TRA LA LA LA LA, TRA LA LA LA LA, THE FLOWERS THAT
> BLOOM IN THE SPRING TRA LA LA LA LA, TRA LA LA LA LA...

JENNIE *is outside, waiting by the church.* **ERIC** *arrives, in running kit, with* **SANDY**, *who's on a bike.*

JENNIE Eric! They're waiting on the pitch for you to run the games. They've been there half an hour.

SANDY If he went as fast as he's supposed to we'd have been on time.

ERIC I'm sorry Jennie.

JENNIE Well sort yourself out and go down there, it'll be dark soon.

ERIC Jennie. Next week.

JENNIE What about it?

ERIC I'll race in London for the first time. It could mean being noticed for the Olympics. We'll get the train to Kings Cross, stay overnight. I'll speak in the morning, before the race. Jennie I want you to come with us, then you can watch, see what it's all about. What do you think?

JENNIE The children's group do the play next week. And the mission has to keep going—

ERIC It would mean a lot to me.

JENNIE I know what running is Eric, I don't need to see it.

ERIC But if you did, I think—

JENNIE You're dashing from one spot to another, what else is there? You're trying to do it faster than the man next to you. It's showing off Eric, it's saying to all those people watching, look at me! I'm the best, I'm the winner, and never mind about the others. It's survival of the fittest, it's battle, it's not what I like and it's not my Eric. I don't need to see it.

ERIC Sandy put your bike away.

SANDY Oh... Aye.

SANDY *goes.*

ERIC It's not a battle.

JENNIE Winners and losers.

ERIC It's a game.

JENNIE Then why's it important?

ERIC God's not sad Jennie. He isn't just devotion and prayer. He wants us to enjoy life. And I enjoy running. The children's play you're doing. Why's that important?

JENNIE Is Abrahams running?

ERIC *looks at her - amazed.*

ERIC What?

JENNIE Is Abrahams running in London?

ERIC Yes. Yes he is but how did you—

JENNIE Well then. If Abrahams is running, you needn't go. They say he's the best. You might as well stay here.

ERIC Jennie—

Beat.

JENNIE I think we should both go and join the family. In China. That's where we should be.

ERIC I'm still at university.

JENNIE You'll graduate soon enough.

ERIC Jennie I believe God made me for a purpose. And that purpose is China. But he also made me fast, and when I run I feel his pleasure. To win is to honour him... I've got my degree to get, all that work, and then there could be Paris. I'm going to London – I've been noticed now, and if I can train hard enough – yes – it could be the *Olympic Games*.

This means little to her.

And you're right, at the moment, I'm letting everyone down. There's not enough of me. You, the mission. I can't do all I could before.

So I want you to look after it for me. My work here. Let me focus on getting to the Olympics. Then I'll be back, with my degree, and we'll both go to China, together.

Please. What do you think?

A moment.

JENNIE I'm frightened.

ERIC Frightened? Frightened of what?

JENNIE You do what you have to Eric. I've got my work to get to. The meals for the families, the shipworkers. Not everyone has the luxury to run Eric. If I'm not there, they'll starve.

ABRAHAMS *strides in, with a swirl of train smoke and city air, and he starts to get ready for the race.* SYBIL *enters in a coat and hat, with a newspaper.*

SYBIL Front page – The Flying Scotsman! They say he's going to show you a thing or two!

She kisses him as ERIC *enters with* SANDY, *who is reading the same paper. They've just got off the train.*

SANDY The Flying Scotsman comes south to tackle the cream of Cambridge!

They'll read that and be quaking in their boots!

SANDY *and* ERIC *start getting ready for the race on one side, in the changing room.* ABRAHAMS *is on the other, joined by* AUBREY *and* ANDY.

AUBREY Have you seen the crowd? All of London's turned out.

ANDY I was at the Garrick last night. Worried I'm still a bit tight.

AUBREY Harold wasn't out drinking. Were you? Harold! Last minute circuits round Paddington Rec I expect.

HAROLD *doesn't hear them. He's dressing, carefully focusing.*

ANDY Whatever it takes Aubrey. Harold can do what he likes. Just so long as he *wins*.

ERIC Mr Abrahams?

ERIC *has walked over, and caught* HAROLD *by surprise. He turns. The two of them meet. Centre stage. For the first time.* ERIC *puts out his hand.* HAROLD *takes it.*

HAROLD Mr Liddell.

ERIC I'd like to wish you the very best of success.

HAROLD Thank you. And may the best man win.

They smile and go back to their sides.

And then – a roar from the CROWD *and the scene is set for the race. People in the stands –* SYBIL, SANDY. *The runners line up.* HAROLD, ERIC *and four others.*

ERIC Dear Jennie.

HAROLD Dear Dad...

They take their places, and slowly start jogging, somehow they can run on the spot.

When you race it's like time slows down.

ERIC You feel every muscle, every moment of the race—

HAROLD Every point is a second—

ERIC You could tell a story of it—

HAROLD Every second a minute.

ERIC When you dig the start, when you see the others—

HAROLD Something happens—

The ~~treadmills~~ underneath them are getting faster and faster...

ERIC A hundred metres can feel like a marathon. You crouch...

HAROLD You wait...

ERIC From the corner of your eye, the gun—

They're running...

STARTER On your marks.

They're running – readying themselves...

Set...

Bracing...

Go!

The gun is fired and the six of them now run full pelt. Very, very fast...

It goes on for longer than a hundred metres... A larger flipping score board – like an old cricket scoreboard counts the metres...

Ten

ABRAHAMS *rolling his arms, and upper body.*

Twenty

LIDDELL *all over the place. It's neck and neck at first...*

Thirty

The determination...

Forty

All of the them, flat out...

Fifty

Then suddenly, ERIC*'s head goes back, and he takes the lead.*

Sixty

HAROLD *aware of this in the corner of his eye.*

Seventy

Nearly there...

Eighty

HAROLD *snatches a look across at* ERIC, *just as they get to the line—*

Ninety...

And ERIC *smashes through first.*

One hundred!

SANDY You did it, Eric, you did it!

ANDY Extraordinary.

The CROWD *erupts in a huge cheer.* SANDY *and most of the* CROWD *rush onto the pitch and lift* ERIC *above them, cheering, and carry him away. The other athletes drift off, until it's just* HAROLD.

HAROLD *sits...utterly distraught.*

SYBIL *enters. Looks at him for a moment.*

SYBIL Gosh Harold, it's not like anybody's died. It was a race and you lost. It happens all the time.

HAROLD Not to me.

SYBIL You were fast, but he was faster, that's all there is to it.

HAROLD I looked. In that last moment. It's the first rule of the whole thing, you never look, but with thirty yards to go, I could feel him taking it so I glanced over and then, in that second...

SYBIL There was nothing you could've done. He won. Fair and square. Now how about a drink? Andy's laid on a party—

HAROLD So that's that Abrahams, all over.

SYBIL Well if you can't take a beating, maybe it's for the best.

HAROLD I don't run to be beaten, I run to win. Anyway it's not the losing. Liddell's a fine man and a fine runner – it's me. All that work, wasted. What do I aim for now?

SYBIL Beating him next time—

HAROLD I can't! I can't run any faster! I wanted the Olympics, I can't even beat the fastest in the country. You don't understand! How could you? How could you possibly understand anything that I do?

He's never spoken to her like that before.

SYBIL He warned me.

HAROLD Who?

SYBIL Tim. When we started seeing each other, he took me aside and said you were a wonderful runner, but as a brother-in-law you'd be a total disaster. He told me to stay away. Now I see what he meant.

She goes. DSR

Stand
HAROLD Sybil... Sybil!

But she's gone. He stands and kicks the ground. Furious.

VOICE Mr Abrahams?

HAROLD *looks up, it's* **SAM**.

HAROLD Oh no...you saw it?

SAM Just heard you talking to that young lady about the Olympics.

HAROLD No. You were right. I'm a fool. I'm sorry. I'll leave you alone. I'll leave the whole bloody thing...

SAM I can find you another two yards.

HAROLD *looks up at him. A projector is wheeled on.*

HAROLD What?

SAM You want to beat Liddell?

Another two yards. Then you'd stand a chance.

Part Four

SAM switches a switch and the room changes to flickering projector light. HAROLD *picks himself up, as* SAM *talks.*

A very fit, good-looking man, in running gear, appears and stands in the light. PADDOCK.

SAM Charlie Paddock. The Californian Cannonball. World's fastest human. Winner 100 metres Olympic Games Antwerp 1920. Time?

HAROLD Er... Ten point three.

PADDOCK Yup.

PADDOCK *stands to the side and is replaced by* JACKSON SCHOLZ.

SAM Jackson Scholz, the New York Thunderbolt, runner up Olympic Games 1920 – he lost by looking right... Have a look—

SCHOLZ *and* PADDOCK *calmly arrange themselves into the finishing position.* SAM *walks up to them and shows* HAROLD.

You see. He's about to jump at the tape, and Scholz is looking. That glance cost him the race.

~~SAM pats SCHOLZ on the back and they relax. Stand to the side.~~

Scholz's fastest?

HAROLD Ten point...five?

SCHOLZ Four.

SAM Learn them.

ERIC *appears in the light.*

Eric Liddell. Well. You know all about him. Look at them. All of them. They never leave you alone. I want their faces leering at you every time you shut your eyes.

HAROLD ~~goes up to~~ **LIDDELL**.

HAROLD The Flying Scotsman. That bloody well hurt.

SAM Liddell's no problem. He's a great runner, but he's not a hundred metres man. His arms swinging round, and that head of his, when it goes back. He's fast but he won't go faster, not in the dash anyway, he's all heart, digs deep – but a short sprint is run on nerves. You got nerves Harold?

HAROLD Paddock, Scholz, Liddell.

They go away as **SAM** *switches on the light.*

SAM Come here.

They meet in the middle.

Why do you think you lost the other day? Because you looked?

HAROLD Yes.

SAM No. Because Liddell's got something you haven't? Not a bit of it.

You're over-striding – just a couple of inches. You're losing power, balance. Look!

~~Ten runners dressed as~~ **HAROLD** ~~enter~~.

~~Here. Your strides over the hundred metres course. Look!~~

~~They line up across the course.~~

As I said – over-striding. Death to the sprinter. Slap in the face each stride you take.

~~The Harolds all start to leave. The first~~ He *slaps* **HAROLD**.

HAROLD Hey!

The second does the same.

SAM Every stride—

The third.

SAM – a mistake.

HAROLD Stop!

The fourth – **HAROLD** *grabs his arm – stops the slap.*

SAM Good. You want to do something about it. You want to run in the Olympics, these selectors you want them to notice you. Yes. *Good!* Let's see if we can fit one more in there. Shorten your stride.

Two more appear – take their places. The others have to shuffle in a little.

SAM So!

Demonstrate

The foremost Harold sprints off round the track.

Perfect. Balance. Power.

The Harolds leave. **JENNIE** *enters, with soup and some vegetables, working hard.*

So. Imagine you're running on hot bricks. Boiling hot! You leave your feet down too long you get burnt.

HAROLD Like this? Runs on spot.

SAM Run over the ground, not into it. Over the ground, not into it. Now, sprint! A Exit DS elsewhere exit

HAROLD *and* **SAM** *leave training, as a footman enters with a hurdle. He sets it up, as we transform to* **LORD LINDSEY***'s country house. Beautiful sunlight.* **ANDY** *and* **SYBIL** *in glorious summer dress, on the lawn.*

ANDY Oh Syb, Harold is a bull, we all know that, but it's probably that same thing that attracted you to him in the first place. The determination!

SYBIL Yes but with me, he was different. Now I've lost him. Every weekend he's away at some other event. And this new coach. It's always The Olympic Games, the few times I see him, it's all he talks about.

ANDY Well old girl that's what he's like. As far as he's concerned, he's going to be there and he has to win, that's all there is to it. Champagne please Foster. The 1902.

FOSTER The 1902 sir? We only have a single bottle of—

ANDY Precisely Foster, that's the chap. Off you go.

FOSTER Hmm.

> **FOSTER** *reluctantly goes.*

ANDY Syb, he loves you.

SYBIL He says I'm a distraction.

ANDY And so you are, what a view! Enough to put any man off his stride.

You have to understand he's preparing for the moment of his life! The world's against him – or so he believes – and now's his chance to *prove* himself. To everyone. Yes, every evening, when he trains, and every weekend, in competition.

SYBIL So the lady must wait.

ANDY I'm sure he would agree the lady can do what she likes. But under it all he's head and heels for you Syb. And dare I say it, I think you feel the same.

> *The footman re-enters with the champagne bottle and two glasses. He shows the bottle to* **ANDY**.

Thank you Foster.

FOSTER You're certain about this, sir?

ANDY Absolutely.

Over the next, the footman puts two champagne glasses on the edge of the hurdle.

SYBIL Well what about you and Aubrey? Neither of you have changed like that. And you both want to win. Isn't the chance there for you too?

ANDY Oh to be fast yes. But not the *fastest*. Faster than any man ever before. That's immortality. And think what that would mean to Harold in particular. It's life and death all this, to him. The stuff of existence. But for me, the whole thing's just fun. I have to try my damnedest to make it mean anything at all.

The footman has finished.

Don't worry Syb. I've never seen a man so bitten. Unfortunately for me. I thought it was the Irish that get all the luck. Are you staying for dinner?

He takes off his robe – he's wearing his running gear.

SYBIL I'm on stage at eight.

ANDY Of course! How could I forget? Evans'll drive you.

SYBIL Dare I ask, Andy – what are you doing?

ANDY Ah – little trick of mine. When hurdling, one is supposed to clear them as low as possible, without making a touch. So here's the arrangement – we fill these chaps on here, then I go for it, aim as close as possible. If I spill a drop Foster gets the rest of the bottle, but if I clear, I down it myself. Usually we go for the shameful stuff in the cellar, but speaking to you Syb, I've realised you're right. It has to *matter*. So...

He takes the bottle from FOSTER *– shows it to* SYBIL.

The 1902. My father ordered it when I was born. Said to crack it open on a special occasion.

SYBIL Oh Andy!

ANDY Means rather a lot to us both. Be a shame to spill it on the turf wouldn't it? So...

He cracks open the bottle, then gives it to **FOSTER**, *who fills the glasses.*

I have a bash at this every day at the moment. Sometimes I do it. Sometimes I don't. Must be a bit like you on stage Syb. Slightly different every night yes?

SYBIL Quite.

ANDY Alright then!

He steadies himself, then runs at the hurdle. The actor really attempts it. Maybe he achieves it. Maybe he doesn't. Either way, **FOSTER** *ends up with a glass of champagne.*

ANDY Have a good show Syb! Break a leg!

HAROLD *enters as* **FOSTER** *clears the hurdle offstage.* **HAROLD** *wears evening dress, and is finishing the tie as he waits to go in, anxious.* **AUBREY** *enters, reading a paper.*

HAROLD Any news?

AUBREY Not yet. But it'll be tonight. Andy's having it telegraphed, and run over. We'll know as soon as they announce. The Olympic team! It could be us. Nerve racking, isn't it! What are you doing?

HAROLD Waiting.

AUBREY Waiting? What for?

The **MASTER OF CAIUS** *enters with a drink, and one for* **HAROLD**.

CAIUS Ah, Mr Abrahams, how good of you to join us.

AUBREY I should go. Good luck old man.

The **MASTER OF TRINITY** *enters with a drink of his own, and we're in their private dining room.*

CAIUS Laid this down in 1914, the day of the declaration. Hard to credit now, the optimism then, the faith in our shared purpose.

TRINITY The prevailing spirit it was.

CAIUS Cambridge was buoyant. A call to arms, and these young men responded, like no one would believe. But you've served us well Abrahams. Those who've built on their sacrifice. Yours is a fine generation. Outstanding in its promise.

HAROLD Thank you sir.

CAIUS They will rest in peace, with what you will do, I am sure of it.

HAROLD *smiles, graciously.*

TRINITY This fine old university. She offers some rare consolations, wouldn't you say, Abrahams?

HAROLD I would sir. Consolations beyond measure.

TRINITY We take it therefore that you would be concerned to discover that some action, or behaviour on your part was causing her grief?

HAROLD Yes sir. Deeply.

A moment. The glass is topped up. The flames flicker.

TRINITY At Cambridge, we have long believed that our games are indispensible. They help mould the complete Englishman – character, courage, honesty and leadership. They demonstrate the importance of duty, of working for a common goal.

HAROLD Yes sir.

TRINITY But I am afraid there have been voices Abrahams. A growing suspicion in the bosom of the university – and I tell you this without in any way decrying your achievements

– that, in your enthusiasm to succeed, you have perhaps lost sight of these ideals.

HAROLD *looks at him.*

HAROLD Suspicions.

TRINITY Indeed. You have surely heard rumours.

HAROLD Of course. This is Cambridge. But this is not simply suspicion. The word grief was mentioned. May I ask what causes this grief?

TRINITY Abrahams, subtlety is lost on you, is it not?

HAROLD I have been taught to speak openly, to bring suspicion and rumour to the surface. So if I may ask again—

CAIUS You have a personal trainer, do you not?

HAROLD Mr Mussabini yes.

TRINITY Mussabini – is he Italian?

HAROLD Of Italian extraction yes—

TRINITY I see—

HAROLD But not all Italian—

TRINITY I'm relieved to hear it.

HAROLD He's half Arab.

TRINITY MASTER *coughs slightly and turns away.*

CAIUS And you employ this Mussabini on a professional basis?

HAROLD Sam Mussabini is the finest, most advanced athletics coach in the country.

CAIUS But he is a professional?

HAROLD He knows what he's doing.

CAIUS A professional.

HAROLD Of course! He's the best! What else would he be?

TRINITY Ah. Well. This is where we part company. Abrahams, we at Cambridge believe in the way of the amateur.

HAROLD I am an amateur.

TRINITY You are trained by a professional. You adopt a professional approach. You do not attend to your academic study as you might – for the past year you have concentrated wholly on developing your own technique, in the pursuit, it seems clear to all, of individual glory. I, and many others, look at Harold Abrahams, and fail to find the loyalty and comradeship – we see instead a man with a single vision and no thought for anything except the applause he receives at the end, the column inches in the newspaper, the number of "autographs". Is this a noble purpose? Truly?

HAROLD I am a Cambridge man, first and last. I am an Englishman first and last. What I have achieved, what I will achieve, is for my university and my country and I bitterly resent your suggesting otherwise.

A flicker between them—

CAIUS Your aim, is it not, is to win at all costs?

HAROLD At all costs no. But I do aim to win within the rules. Perhaps you would rather I played the gentleman and lost.

CAIUS To playing the tradesman – yes!

A pause. They calm a little. A certain admiration for the young man – despite everything...

TRINITY My boy. Your approach has been, shall we say, a little too plebian. You are the elite, and must behave as such.

HAROLD *looks at his glass.*

HAROLD I can see gentlemen, that you yearn for victory, just as I do. But achieved with the apparent effortlessness of the Gods. Yours are the archaic values of the prep school playground, and the world is throwing them off. We know that success of any kind, real success, does not come with ease, with grace, it requires *effort*, passion, a dignity that comes with relentless, *graft*, with *work*. I believe in the pursuit of excellence of this kind, and I know, gentlemen, I can see ever so clearly, the future is with me. I will race in the Olympics, and I will win.

Good evening.

He hands glass to **TRINITY** *and steps away, leaving, but staying separate on stage.*

TRINITY There you have it Hugh. Your Semite departs. A different God – a different mountaintop.

They go...leaving **HAROLD** *on his own, outside in the courtyard. Pumped up - passionate - angry.*

HAROLD Barukh ata Adonai Eloheinu Melekh ha-olam, asher kid'shanu b'mitzvotav v'tzivanu l'hadlik ner shel Shabbat. Barukh ata Adonai Eloheinu Melekh ha-olam, asher kid'shanu b'mitzvotav v'tzivanu l'hadlik ner shel Shabbat. Barukh ata Adonai Eloheinu Melekh ha-olam, asher kid'shanu b'mitzvotav v'tzivanu l'hadlik ner shel Shabbat!

He turns - sees **ERIC LIDDELL** *standing...*

Life is simple for you isn't it?

ERIC Never simple, no.

HAROLD You've a father who loves you though.

ERIC Aye.

HAROLD Who's proud.

ERIC Yes. I believe he is, yes.

Beat.

HAROLD Sometimes I feel like writing to suggest we meet. Just the two of us, on a track, early in the morning. I'd show you. I'd beat you. Eric Liddell. Once and for all.

ERIC Why do you run?

HAROLD I beg your pardon.

ERIC Why do you run Harold?

HAROLD The same reason as you. To win.

ERIC To win what?

The race?

A long pause.

Then... **AUBREY**'s *voice from off.* ~~DSL → Ame~~

AUBREY Harold! Harold!

He comes running on stage with a piece of paper.

We're in!

HAROLD What?

SANDY *runs on.* ~~DSR → Eric~~

SANDY Eric!

AUBREY You one hundred and two hundred, Andy four hundred and hurdles, and me the steeplechase.

Paris here we come!

SANDY You're on the team. One hundred metres.

AUBREY Eric Liddell's picked too – rivals under the same flag. Harold! The Olympic Games!

ERIC Abrahams?

SANDY Yes.

AUBREY This is your chance to get even.

ERIC Yes.

ABRAHAMS I can't wait! ~~Face CS look at Eric~~

ABRAHAMS *and* **LIDDELL** *looking at each other.*

Fade on the scene – then with a huge boom.

House light – and the Olympic logo for the first time. White on black.

Large and over the whole theatre.

Interval

ACT TWO

Part One

The stage is flooded with **CROWDS – REPORTERS** *– flash-bulbs, and banners – luggage being loaded.*

We're at Dover, in celebratory mood – there is a gangplank up to the ferry – which is a miniature, complete version of a vessel – there is a channel through the **CROWD** *to it. Once they go inside, they make their way to the top deck of the boat and wave.*

There's cheering – the first to appear is **LORD BIRKENHEAD**. *A cigar and slicked black hair. Loves the showbiz of it all.*

REPORTER Sir! Sir! Lord Birkenhead! Many people are saying that British athletics is a lost cause—

BIRKENHEAD What people?

REPORTER That compared to the professionally-trained Charlie Paddock and Jackson Schultz, our boys don't stand a chance – do you care to comment?

BIRKENHEAD *laughs, loudly.*

BIRKENHEAD Yes well while it's certainly true that the Americans have prepared specially, some might say *too* specially to gain success, we feel that in our unsophisticated way we have their match.

REPORTER Will the weather make a difference?

BIRKENHEAD I'm sure the Americans have developed a special procedure for every meteorological eventuality, but we British have our own tried and tested method.

REPORTER What's that sir?

BIRKENHEAD We bloody well get on with it.

REPORTER But the Americans—

BIRKENHEAD Abrahams, Liddell and Lindsey. Those are the names to watch. And let me tell you, they aren't worried about a thing.

He goes onto the boat. **ANDY** *arrives, with a trolley and a footman both stacked with luggage. He meets* **AUBREY**, *who has one suitcase.*

AUBREY Gosh Andy, it's Paris we're headed, not Peru.

ANDY Aubrey, there are certain standards – you know who's going to be there, don't you?

AUBREY Who?

ANDY The Prince of Wales.

AUBREY I beg your pardon?!

ANDY He's very much looking forward to meeting us, apparently.

AUBREY But what am I going to do? I only brought one pair of trousers!

They get on the boat as **ERIC** *arrives with* **SANDY**.

ERIC Has Jennie said anything to you? She's a good girl I know but—

SANDY Never you mind about Jennie. Keep your focus.

ERIC It's good of you to see me off Sandy, but you have to stay over there.

SANDY Why?

ERIC This is just for people getting on the boat.

SANDY Aye, I know, that's me.

ERIC You? We're not allowed personal trainers.

SANDY I'm not your trainer, I'm your valet. Come on!

They walk up towards the ferry. The REPORTERS *shout!*
Flashbulbs.

REPORTER 2 Mr Liddell!

He waves.

What do you think your chances are? Against Mr Abrahams?

ERIC I'll do my best!

REPORTER 3 What about Sunday?

ERIC What?

REPORTER 3 Do you think you can beat the Americans in the
heat on Sunday?

ERIC *turns to* SANDY.

ERIC Sunday?

SANDY It's in the papers this morning. The whole programme.
The heats are on the Sunday after the opening ceremony.

ERIC *just stares – the blood draining out of him.*

Eric! It's only a heat.

I thought you knew.

ERIC No...

SANDY Come on. We'll talk on board...

They go inside. Other Olympic athletes go in.

HAROLD *arrives with his luggage. On his own. The*
REPORTERS *see him.*

REPORTER Mr Abrahams! Harold! What do you think? Will you win? Will you beat Eric Liddell?

HAROLD I'm confident.

REPORTER Confident? Good. Good luck!

SYBIL Harold...

HAROLD sees SYBIL, who's standing there.

HAROLD Sybil...

He takes her aside and they talk...

SYBIL I had to see you off didn't I?

HAROLD But I haven't written.

SYBIL I know.

HAROLD Or seen you – oh Syb, I've been a beast. How did you even know where to come?

SYBIL Andy. He said you'd be pleased. I wanted to wish you luck.

HAROLD And everything's going well is it? What are you on to at the moment?

SYBIL Pirates of Penzance.

HAROLD Pirates! When I'm back Syb. I'll be there. I promise.

SYBIL You will win, won't you Harold?

HAROLD I...well... I...don't—

SYBIL Harold? I wanted you to know. I understand. I do. And I'll be there, when you get back. I checked and your train gets into Victoria at half past four, so I'll be there, at the station, waiting.

HAROLD Syb—

SYBIL After you've won.

*They smile. The **HARBOUR MASTER** is making the final preparations for the boat to sail.*

HARBOUR MASTER Hurry please Mr Abrahams, she's about to sail.

SYBIL Write.

HAROLD Of course.

SYBIL Not to me. Your father.

HAROLD Oh.

SYBIL And send it. This time. Harold.

Don't let him just read about it in the newspapers, with everyone else.

HARBOUR MASTER All aboard!

HAROLD kisses SYBIL and then runs onto the boat. Lots of waving! Cheering. The ship sounds its siren. The anchor is lifted, streamers cut. Someone plays the run up of Gilbert and Sullivan.

The sides collapse and we see inside. Little cabins and moments. Some people writing letters, others eating, a bar with a piano where people are singing.

CHORUS

COME FRIENDS WHO PLOUGH THE SEA!
TRUCE TO NAVIGATION! TAKE ANOTHER STATION!
LET'S VARY PIRACY. WITH A LITTLE BURGLARY!

COME FRIENDS WHO PLOUGH THE SEA!
TRUCE TO NAVIGATION! TAKE ANOTHER STATION!
LET'S VARY PIRACY. WITH A LITTLE...

As everyone gathers in the bar – **LORD BIRKENHEAD** *taps a glass for attention...*

BIRKENHEAD Gentlemen. We are all on our way, all on board this fine vessel, you look wonderful in your finery so no disasters yet! However I have been asked if you would, once we arrive in Paris, save your sartorial splendour, at least until after the opening ceremony. Like our athletes, we have no replacements, so I urge you to look after your uniforms and yourselves...

ALL
WITH CAT-LIKE TREAD, UPON OUR PREY WE STEAL
IN SILENCE DREAD, OUR CAUTIOUS WAY WE FEEL
NO SOUND AT ALL, WE NEVER SPEAK A WORD,
A FLY'S FOOT FALL, WOULD BE DISTINCTLY HEARD.

ERIC stands and slightly in another world moves away from the **CHORUS**.

BIRKENHEAD Gentlemen, you are the chosen few. The best this country has to offer. The most powerful athletic force ever to leave these shores. You will face the world's best, fleet of foot and strong of limb, from every civilised nation on the face of the earth. I am in no doubt you will acquit yourselves not only honourably, but with distinction.

CHORUS
COME FRIENDS WHO PLOUGH THE SEA!

All continue humming, as **ERIC** *moves even further apart.*

The piano run up – and then silence! **HAROLD, ANDY, AUBREY** *and* **LIDDELL** *all facing out.*

ANDY Dear Papa – it's simply thrilling to be here at last. Wonderful to all be in it together. All for one, and one for all!

HAROLD Father, this is the proudest day, to represent one's country, to the world! To show them all, who we are, what we stand for, this must be what you dreamed of when you came to Britain.

AUBREY I wish you could see us Ma, the wonderful spirit abroad now we've left England. There's not a chap amongst us who isn't ready to burst his heart for all we've left behind.

CHORUS

COME FRIENDS WHO PLOUGH THE SEA!
TRUCE TO NAVIGATION! TAKE ANOTHER STATION!
LET'S VARY PIRACY. WITH A LITTLE BURGLARY!

ERIC ...

BIRKENHEAD Are you sure, Liddell?

The other men leave **LIDDELL** *on stage, with* **BIRKENHEAD,** *on the deck.*

Because when I received the news, I couldn't quite believe it. Hundreds of young men, who'd love to be in your shoes, aboard this vessel, the symbol of national pride – and you reject it, your country, and your duty. You must've known this was possible?

ERIC It never occurred to me – running on a Sunday...

BIRKENHEAD Liddell. Yourself and Abrahams, you're our key men, and the whole of Britain is watching, hoping. When they hear about this, I'm not sure the people will understand. I'm not sure that I understand.

ERIC I know sir, I've given up so much to be on this ship. My studies have suffered, my place on the national rugby team, I've hurt someone dear to me. All because I told myself that if I won, I would win for God, in his name. But now, I find myself standing here and...

To run would be against his will.

BIRKENHEAD *looks at him.*

BIRKENHEAD Hmm. Well. As things stand you must not run. But hold fire for a while, leave it to me. I'll have a word with the French. They're not entirely unreasonable – God knows we fought in the war together – they do owe us something. Wouldn't you say?

ERIC I don't know—

BIRKENHEAD They don't hold much with principle the Frogs, but they're proud. They won't want a fuss.

Yes. I might just persuade them.

ERIC Of what?

BIRKENHEAD To move that bloody heat of yours of course.

The siren sounds.

The sound of a foghorn – a banner drops "La VIII Olympiade – Bienvenue à tous – Citius Altius Fortius" and out of the boat processes the British Olympic team.

To join – a much bigger procession – two people represent each country – a name in French and a flag. Although in reality there were forty-four, we see twenty – but it still looks like a lot. The twenty we see (all in French) are...

Argentina, Bulgaria, Canada, Cuba, France, Great Britain, Haiti, Ireland, Japan, Latvia, New Zealand, Poland, South Africa, Egypt, Mexico, Luxumburg, Yugoslavia.

They enter and line up, facing the presidential box, where **THE PRINCE OF WALES** *is sat with the Head of the Olympic Committee and the French President.*

In the middle of the procession a strange podium is erected – draped in the Olympic flag. On this, climbs **GEORGES ANDRE** *a famous French athlete, who then, with his arm outstretched, delivers the Athletes' Oath...*

GEORGES Nous jurons, dit-il, que nous nous présentons aux Jeux Olympiques en concurrents loyaux, respectueux des règlements qui les régissent et désireux d'y participer dans un esprit chevaleresque pour l'honneur de nos pays et la gloire du sport.

The French national anthem, a wave of the flag – **AUBREY,** **ANDY, HAROLD** *and* **ERIC** *are stood together.*

HAROLD Where are they?

AUBREY What?

HAROLD Paddock. Scholz.

AUBREY I beg your pardon?

ERIC The Americans...

And on cue, the other teams move back to reveal – the American team. They're training – very fit, being pushed as hard as they can by their trainers who shout at them.

AUBREY Gosh.

HAROLD They've got their own set of houses, their own training ground, been here a week already, and apparently they had special tracks built on the boat over, so they could keep fit on the way. Look at them! Now that's training! They *mean it.*

HAROLD, ANDY, AUBREY *and* **ERIC** *stare at the Americans training. One of them,* **CHARLES PADDOCK,** *moves to the centre.*

There they are – Charlie Paddock. Jackson Scholz.

AUBREY Got your plate full there Harold.

HAROLD These men work every hour of the day, their approach is scientific, relentless, methodical...

ANDY How dreary...

HAROLD Charlie Paddock.

Jackson Scholz.

You know what they call them?

SCHOLZ *runs on the spot, extremely fast.* **HAROLD** *turns to* **ERIC.**

The fastest men in the world.

An **ANNOUNCER** *steps forward with a megaphone.*

ANNOUNCER Four hundred metres hurdles. Le quatre-cents metres haies.

ANDY Alright then. Off we go.

One by one they congratulate him and leave.

HAROLD Good luck old man.

AUBREY All the best.

ANDY Thanks.

> **ANDY** *is left with the other competitors. They line up on the tread. Cheering from the* **CROWD**.

TANNOY Pret!

The official holds the gun and then...

Fires it.

> **ANDY** *runs like hell. Then jumps! Lands on the treadmill and keeps on the running...jumps again... The clapperboard counts...as before fifty metres, one hundred metres, one-hundred-and-fifty metres.*

It's a feat of athletics jumping on the tread, landing and running...he doesn't look to the side...jumps again... Two-hundred-and-fifty metres..

Three hundred.

Three-hundred-and-fifty...

Four hundred!

> **ANDY** *jumps off the treadmill and lands...*

AUBREY Silver! It's a silver! Congratulations old man. Silver!

> *A huge cheer!* **HAROLD** *and* **AUBREY** *and others run over to congratulate him as he recovers...*

ERIC *hangs back – sees* BIRKENHEAD – *who looks at him disapprovingly.* SANDY *runs over—*

SANDY Eric – our first medal! We're going for a drink to celebrate – a few of us.

ERIC I'll join you later on.

SANDY *looks at him.*

SANDY It'll be alright you know. They'll find a way round it. Course they will.

ERIC Have a good time.

go to Juliet with Sean

And off he goes, leaving ERIC *on his own.* FLORENCE *appears – looking round. Lost.*

Are you alright?

FLORENCE Where's the way out?

ERIC Over there.

FLORENCE Oh – great – thanks – Hey... Mr Liddell? Eric Liddell.

ERIC Aye.

FLORENCE Florence Mackenzie. Seen your picture in the newspapers. Pleased to meet you.

They shake hands.

ERIC Mackenzie's a Scottish name.

FLORENCE Do I sound Scottish?

ERIC American.

FLORENCE Canadian. Eric Liddell. The minister in our church back home talks about you all the time. How you read from the bible before meetings. He says you run for God. I like that. I came over to see my friend Anne-Marie, and saw about the games. Thought I'd take a look. Is everything alright?

ERIC I...

ERIC *gets a pen out.*

It's good to meet you Florence. But I have to be going—

FLORENCE What are you doing?

ERIC If you'd like me to sign—

FLORENCE Eric, I don't want an autograph. It's just great to meet you. Why are you here, all on your own? The others are off celebrating.

ERIC You're not with anyone.

FLORENCE Anne-Marie's not interested. She said running's for children and hamsters.

She reaches into her bag.

But I don't agree, so I came on my own. Here. This is where I'm staying, perhaps we could have dinner?

ERIC My friend Sandy told me Americans were confident, I see what he means.

FLORENCE I'm Canadian Eric, you'll get it eventually. We could even discuss your problem if you wanted.

ERIC What problem?

FLORENCE Something's the matter and you're not telling anyone. Right?

She looks at him. Somehow she knows.

Up to you. But you're a good man. There aren't many of those. So if I can help? Good to meet you Eric.

ERIC You too.

They smile – she's about to go.

Er... There's a reception tonight. We could meet for dinner and then you could come with me, afterwards. If you wanted?

They look at each other.

FLORENCE Yes, I'd like that.

VP or Juliet

High up, through a window we see a small room. **SAM MUSSABINI** *looks out.* **HAROLD** *in the background.*

HAROLD How was your journey?

SAM Economical. Had a drink. Passed the time. So that's the stadium is it?

HAROLD Well the top of it, yes.

SAM I can see the flagpole. Suppose that's all I'll need. One way or another.

HAROLD It's as good as being there.

SAM Better, seeing as I'm persona non grata—

HAROLD I'm sorry Sam, it's ridiculous, that we're not allowed trainers. We could buy you a ticket, you could watch at least?

SAM Best not lad. Cause a distraction. To you and everyone else. I'll stay here. It's good.

He tests the bed.

Yes. Tip top Mr Abrahams. If we don't win now, we never will. All we both want now, is a good night's sleep. Keep in shape tomorrow. And you'll be ready. First heat. Show them what you've got. Alright son?

HAROLD *doesn't answer. A moment.*

HAROLD I should have invited him.

SAM Who?

HAROLD My father.

SAM Would he have come all the way over here?

HAROLD Not in a million years.

SAM And you said you've written?

HAROLD Yes.

SAM Well then. Done your best. And it's not about him is it?

HAROLD ...

SAM That's not what you're doing it for.

HAROLD I don't know Sam.

I don't know.

The scene changes in costume and regalia to **BIRKENHEAD***'s reception.* **ANDY** *enters and is spotted by* **THE PRINCE OF WALES.**

PRINCE Lindsey! Congratulations!

ANDY Thank you, Your Highness.

PRINCE I don't know how you did it! I was a complete idiot at hurdles.

ANDY Spot of luck I shouldn't wonder. Sorry it's only a silver.

PRINCE Nonsense! Excellent... Now go and enjoy yourself.

ANDY Thank you sir.

He bows and leaves as **BIRKENHEAD** *approaches, now in black tie himself.*

BIRKENHEAD Your Royal Highness, may I introduce Tom Watson, representing New Zealand.

PRINCE How do you do Mr Watson, you've come a long way.

WATSON I'm at Oxford actually sir. They wrote to me, said as I was over here I might as well take part.

PRINCE Very sensible – but can you run?

WATSON I'll give it a try sir.

PRINCE That's the spirit.

They walk off together to reveal **HAROLD** *and* **AUBREY**, *watching.*

AUBREY He looks different in person. Slightly smaller.

HAROLD It's not the size, Monty, it's the style. You see...no effort at all. That's what he's here to inspire in us. Grace.

ERIC *and* FLORENCE *walk past.*

ERIC I'm sorry about dinner.

FLORENCE Eric it was wonderful. And look at all of this! Good of you to get me in.

ERIC Wasn't difficult, rather short of ladies apparently.

FLORENCE What did you tell them?

ERIC That you're an old friend.

FLORENCE As long as I'm not a distraction.

ERIC You? No, it's not you that's distracting me.

FLORENCE Have they said anything? Have they spoken to the French yet?

ERIC I rather think they hope I'll get to Sunday, forget about it and run.

FLORENCE You have to tell them Eric. You can't just walk around like this smiling and talking to them all as if—

SCHOLZ *has approached.*

SCHOLZ Mr Liddell?

ERIC Yes.

SCHOLZ Jackson Scholz, it's a pleasure.

ERIC Mr Scholz. Pleased to meet you at last.

SCHOLZ Looking forward to the race. The Flying Scotsman, can't wait to see what you can do.

ERIC Oh – can I introduce you? This is a friend of mine. Florence Mackenzie.

SCHOLZ Mackenzie. You're Scottish too.

FLORENCE No—

SCHOLZ My apologies – *British.*

FLORENCE Canadian.

SCHOLZ Well that's British, isn't it?

FLORENCE Not really.

SCHOLZ It's a colony.

FLORENCE A dominion.

SCHOLZ I don't get it.

FLORENCE It's a pleasure to meet you Mr Scholz. A real honour.

> **BIRKENHEAD** *comes over.*

BIRKENHEAD Liddell, I was afraid you weren't here. Do excuse us Mr Scholz, Miss.

FLORENCE Eric. Tell them.

> **BIRKENHEAD** *leads* **ERIC** *away.*

BIRKENHEAD Tell us what Mr Liddell? I hope the news of your predicament hasn't spread...

ERIC No sir, but I do think it's important we have a conversation as soon as possible.

> *The party is clearing.* **BIRKENHEAD** *places* **ERIC** *in a chair, centre stage.*

BIRKENHEAD A conversation?

ERIC Aye.

BIRKENHEAD Well this is a coincidence.

ERIC What do you mean?

BIRKENHEAD Someone else had the very same idea.

ERIC Who?

> *We are now in a private room.*

The PRINCE *enters with* SUTHERLAND *and* CADOGAN.

ERIC No! No I can't.

BIRKENHEAD Your Royal Highness may I present Mr Eric Liddell.

PRINCE Delighted Liddell, delighted. I saw you play for Scotland. Depressed me no end. Ran in a couple of tries from your own half I remember.

ERIC I believe I did sir, yes.

PRINCE Still, we're on the same side now eh?

ERIC Yes sir.

BIRKENHEAD Eric, may I introduce His Grace the Duke of Sutherland President of our Olympic Association.

They shake hands.

ERIC How do you do.

BIRKENHEAD And our chairman, Lord Cadogan.

ERIC *puts his hand out –* CADOGAN *just looks at it.*

Have a seat.

There's one chair. ERIC *has to sit in it. The others stand around him.*

Cigar? Oh. No of course. You don't. Nor drink. Such is the resolution of the young man before us.

A pause.

PRINCE I did enjoy Lindsey's run today. He did well I thought.

ERIC Yes sir. Very well.

Beat.

PRINCE Do you enjoy life? Mr Liddell.

ERIC I try to.

PRINCE Good. Because there are these chaps who feel – I'm sure you've met them – there are these chaps who I can only assume come from a puritan background, and they find no enjoyment in life whatsoever. It's all work for them. It's all suffering. Lord Cadogan thought you might be presenting yourself as one of those.

ERIC I believe in making the most of the life we're given. That means enjoyment of course.

PRINCE Well quite. Good. Have to say you don't seem the sackcloth and ashes sort to me.

ERIC No sir.

PRINCE There you have it, Cadogan. Mr Liddell enjoys life.

CADOGAN Hm!

A beat.

SUTHERLAND The fact of the matter is, Liddell, that Lord Birkenhead has advised us of your attitude toward your participation in the—

CADOGAN Non-participation!

SUTHERLAND Well yes, non-participation – in the hundred metres heat on Sunday.

We were also consulted as to the correct manner in which to approach the French. Something we can't allow to happen, I'm afraid—

CADOGAN Certainly not! Going cap in hand to the Frogs. Out of the question.

SUTHERLAND Yes.

PRINCE Simply a matter of national dignity Liddell. I'm sure you understand.

ERIC Well I must say sir, I felt it was an impractical suggestion from the start.

BIRKENHEAD Then why didn't you bloody well say so man!

ERIC I wanted to run. So when you suggested it sir I—

BIRKENHEAD *I* suggested it?

ERIC Yes sir – after you mentioned the possibility—

BIRKENHEAD I very much doubt I said anything of the sort – approaching the French? For a man of conviction Liddell you're surprisingly slippery.

ERIC I wanted to run. I would still like to run. If there was a solution offered, whoever suggested it, then of course I would take it.

SUTHERLAND Well, all that being understood, we decided to invite you in here to see if there was any way to resolve the situation.

CADOGAN There's only one way to resolve the situation and that's for this young man to change his mind.

PRINCE Don't state the obvious, Cadogan. This young man, I can tell, appreciates subtlety. He is a man of faith and conviction, yes, I do believe that, but I can also see, if you will allow me to say this about you, Mr Liddell, that he is open-minded. He understands the subtle distinction between the domain of ideals and that of practicality. I feel he is an intelligent man, who wants to find a way through all this. Am I right Liddell?

ERIC Sir, if you will allow me to speak frankly—

CADOGAN Who's the woman?

ERIC I... I beg your pardon?

CADOGAN Birkenhead tells us you put a woman on the list at short notice. He tells us you've spent the whole evening with her. Who is she?

SUTHERLAND Lord Cadogan, this isn't—

ERIC She's a friend, not that it's relevant.

CADOGAN I believe it's extremely relevant, this God-fearing young man of conviction has a jolly to Paris and goes off with the first young woman he meets.

ERIC No.

CADOGAN This is not the image of you Liddell, this is not who the public thinks you are. Your position on the race, this woman, it stinks of hypocrisy.

ERIC If you have an accusation to make—

CADOGAN There is a lot of press around Liddell.

Your God... He sees everything.

Beat.

SUTHERLAND Your Highness, I must protest, we are here to talk to Mr Liddell, not threaten him.

PRINCE I agree. But Cadogan has a point.

If your refusal to run were to draw attention Liddell. Well. Many other aspects may emerge.

But if you were simply to compete, as expected...

ERIC I won't run on the Sabbath, sir. I won't. I had intended to confirm this with Lord Birkenhead tonight even before I was pulled up in front of this inquisition of yours.

BIRKENHEAD Hardly an inquisition—

ERIC Aye, you're right, not an inquisition. Blackmail—

CADOGAN Don't be impertinent Liddell.

ERIC The impertinence lies sir with those that seek to influence a man to deny his beliefs.

BIRKENHEAD Absolutely not – it's your beliefs that we're appealing to. In your country.

ERIC No sir.

BIRKENHEAD In your king. Your loyalty to them.

CADOGAN At last, some sense. In my day it was king first and God after.

SUTHERLAND And the war to end wars bitterly proved that point.

CADOGAN Don't you dare, sir!

SUTHERLAND Well I feel this is disgraceful, accusing this man of—

ERIC *is calm – he speaks and for some reason they listen.*

ERIC God made countries. God makes kings, and the rules by which they govern and those rules state that the Sabbath is his. I respect your right to not agree sirs, but I for one intend to keep to my beliefs and keep that day holy.

Beat.

CADOGAN Arrogant. Stubborn.

SUTHERLAND What to do?

They look at the PRINCE. *He moves closer to* ERIC *for the first time.*

PRINCE Mr Liddell you're a child of your race, as am I. We share a common heritage, a common loyalty. There are times when we're asked to make sacrifices in the name of that loyalty. Without them our allegiance is worthless. As I see it, for you, this is such a time.

ERIC Sir, God knows I love my country, but I can't make that sacrifice.

A moment.

PRINCE Forget Cadogan's threats Eric. When this is announced, the people won't care about a woman, they'll feel something much worse. They'll feel betrayed. And it will be that betrayal they will remember. For the rest of your life. Eric Liddell. The man who didn't run. You really will be in God's hands then.

ERIC I know that sir.

But that's my choice.

They look at each other.

SUTHERLAND It appears that we must consider instead how to limit the damage.

PRINCE Yes.

BIRKENHEAD Alright Liddell, if that really is your final word you better leave it to us.

ERIC Yes sir. Your Highness.

ERIC bows. They just watch him as he walks downstage, [DSL] *out of the room. Behind him the officials leave.*

A moment. ERIC getting his breath back.

HAROLD appears behind him. ← CSL behind Eric

HAROLD I asked where you were being led off to. And your friend Sandy told me.

ERIC Harold—

HAROLD He was frantic, hoped I could help sort it all out. Why didn't you tell me?

ERIC They asked me not to.

HAROLD But after coming all the way here? All that training?

ERIC There's nothing I can do Harold. If you have a complaint you can take it up with the—

HAROLD No I'll take it up with you. It's one heat. A single day. You think God's going to care? You think it's going to bother him whether you run on the track or sit in church?

ERIC Aye. I do.

HAROLD Then what kind of God is that? Eric I want to be the fastest in the world. Not the fastest of those that turn up. I can beat you. I can. And I want to prove it.

ERIC You will.

HAROLD Not if you don't run. They'll say I had it easy. They'll write about you as well, say that it's tactical – that you don't want to face me, in case you lose.

ERIC Harold what does any of it mean, if you don't keep hold of what matters?

HAROLD Absolutely. This matters. This race.

ERIC Only this?

Why do you run Harold?

A beat.

HAROLD Same reason as you. To win.

ERIC No.

Pause.

Harold, I was faster than you in London I know, but you've seen the recent times. You're faster, you'd beat me, we both know it already. It's Scholz, Paddock, that's who you need to worry about—

HAROLD But we can't be certain. After these Games they say you're stopping.

ERIC Aye.

HAROLD For good.

ERIC That's right.

HAROLD So we'll never know. If you don't compete, that's it. No one will ever be certain who would have won. Between you and me. Who was faster. No one will ever know.

ERIC And I'm sorry for that Harold. But this is what matters to me.

HAROLD ...

ERIC You do respect that?

HAROLD ...

ERIC Harold?

> ERIC *holds out his hand.*

> HAROLD *looks at it.*

This is the stuff of life Harold. The unexpected challenge.

> HAROLD *takes his hand.*

It's just you now. *Keep it*

The moment is broken by ANDY *who enters, with* FLORENCE.

ANDY Ah! Got you both together. Good. How are you Eric? Any progress?

ERIC No. I won't run. That's it.

ANDY We thought as much didn't we?

FLORENCE Yes.

ANDY Man of principal. Can't argue with that. But as it happens all's not lost because Florence here has had a rather clever idea. And we thought if you two were on board, we go in front of the high council, give it a whirl. Alright? Harold? We could do with your support?

HAROLD What's the idea?

> *The committee re-enter as* ANDY *speaks.*

ANDY Gentlemen: another day, another race.

CADOGAN What the hell is that supposed to mean?

ANDY It's quite simple as a matter of fact, sir. The four hundred metres. It's on Thursday. I've already got my medal, so why don't we let Eric take my place?

> *A moment, the room is unsure.*

BIRKENHEAD What do you think Liddell?

ERIC I'm flattered they'd offer it...

CADOGAN It's not his event. He doesn't stand a chance.

BIRKENHEAD Abrahams. Do you have a view?

Beat.

HAROLD Of course I'm disappointed not to compete against him but... I do believe Eric's our best, sir, in any race.

The men look at each other.

SUTHERLAND Can we allow him to change events at such short notice?

CADOGAN That's a matter for the committee.

BIRKENHEAD We are the committee. I think it's a good idea. David?

The **PRINCE** *considers.*

PRINCE Those in favour say "aye".

They do.

And Liddell? Alright with you? Manage the four hundred on Thursday?

ERIC Sir, it's not fair on Lord Lindsey.

ANDY A pleasure old chap. Just to see you run.

ERIC *looks at him.*

ERIC Aye. Thank you.

PRINCE Alright then. Well after all that, I hope you manage to do us proud.

He turns suddenly to **HAROLD**.

Abrahams, looks like when it comes to the sprint, it's all up to you. So how are you feeling? I read that you were confident. I hope so. Get some rest gentlemen. Seems to me, you're going to need it.

Miss Mackenzie. I understand this solution was your idea. Trust the Scots to get us out of a pickle.

FLORENCE I'm not Scottish your Highness.

PRINCE Ah. American. Always found the American accent rather appealing...

FLORENCE Canadian.

PRINCE Oh. Shame.

Begin Training

Part Two

They clear, as **HAROLD** *enters and starts training on the spot.*

ERIC *walks to a pulpit, and speaks. As he walks, we hear the Lord's Prayer in French.*

ERIC My text this afternoon is taken from Isaiah, chapter forty. Behold, the nations are as a drop in a bucket, and are counted as the small dust of the balance. All nations before him are as nothing, and they are counted to him less than nothing and vanity.

AUBREY *enters, soaking, sits in a chair, exhausted and dejected.*

And they that wait upon the Lord shall renew their strength; they shall mount up with wings as eagles, they shall run and not be weary, and they shall walk and not be faint.

HAROLD *finishes training and lies on a bench. He talks to* **AUBREY**.

HAROLD Do you remember that day at Cambridge, Aubrey? When we met, for the very first time. You loaded up with all those cases and tennis rackets and God knows what else. We shared a taxi, went to our rooms. You made me feel like an old hand. I was so superior. Well...

That was the worst miscalculation of my life.

Aubrey.

You are my most complete man.

AUBREY *looks up at him for the first time.*

AUBREY Harold. I tripped. I lost.

HAROLD Kind.

Compassionate.

Brave.

AUBREY Oh Harold.

HAROLD Content.

> **AUBREY** *hears this. It's true. Despite everything he's feeling right now...*

That's your secret. Contentment. I'm twenty-four and I've never known it. I'm always in pursuit, but I don't know what of.

Sam and I, we've worked and worked and laboured and bullied each other. Out rain or shine, when all of you were living your lives, and for what? The heat was a disaster, through by the skin of my teeth, and then the semi – tricked by Paddock like that.

Now in one hour's time I'll be out there again. The final. I'll raise my eyes and look down that corridor, four feet wide, with ten lonely seconds to justify my whole existence.

I wrote to my father, told him all about what was happening, what this meant. But he hasn't replied. He won't.

What am I running for Aubrey? Especially now Liddell's out.

When I get on the track, I'll be lost.

> *He stands. And takes his jacket and kit.*

AUBREY I don't see it like that really. I run to run.

I mean, I'm not like Eric, I'm not at all sure if there's anything to come, you know, *afterwards*. And if not, well it's all about the race isn't it? The here and now. The attempt. I think that's why I do it. The purest thing in the world for me. Achievement. For its own sake.

Good luck Harold.

> **AUBREY** *goes, stands at the side and watches.* **HAROLD** *begins to get dressed, and finds a note in his coat pocket. As he reads,* **SAM** *appears and speaks.*

SAM Dear Mr Abrahams. You must please pardon my not coming to see you run, much as I would like to do so. However, I believe and hope you will win the hundred metres final.

The other competitors enter, readying themselves, getting changed etc, around HAROLD, SCHOLZ *and* PADDOCK, *and* WATSON *and three others.*

Do your best, and don't forget, drop down at the first stride. Get well warmed up and then let the gun release you. I should use the springy old six-spike shoes. All the best of luck from yours truly,

Sam Mussabini.

P.S Please accept the charm. My old father swore by it.

HAROLD *takes the charm, and hangs it round his neck.*

Looks up. Thinks of MUSSABINI...*as he goes...*

Applause. The CROWD *appears – we're outside. The competitors line up.* SANDY *and* ERIC *take their place in the* CROWD *– prominent. The runners are lined up for the inspection by* THE PRINCE OF WALES *and* LORD BIRKENHEAD.

BIRKENHEAD Your Royal Highness, may I present Mr Bowman, of the United States.

PRINCE Mr Bowman.

He bows.

BIRKENHEAD Mr Merchaston.

PRINCE Mr Merchaston.

He bows.

BIRKENHEAD And Mr Watson of New Zealand I believe you know.

PRINCE Ah yes. Mr Watson. How are you?

WATSON Very well sir.

BIRKENHEAD Mr Paddock.

PRINCE Mr Paddock. Dinner for the whole team at my club when we get back to London. You win I pay, Abrahams wins, you pay. Alright?

PADDOCK Sir! You've got yourself a deal!

BIRKENHEAD Mr Scholz, from the United States.

PRINCE Mr Scholz.

BIRKENHEAD And our Mr Abrahams.

PRINCE Good luck Abrahams. Do your best – that's all we can expect.

HAROLD Thank you sir.

PRINCE Gentlemen.

The PRINCE *and* BIRKENHEAD *make their way back to the stand as the* RUNNERS *line up.*

STARTER To your marks! *middle lane*

The RUNNERS *get in position. The clapperboard is there…*

SAM Head down…watch that first stride.

AUBREY Go on Harold.

ANDY Go on…

ERIC Your best Harold.

HAROLD *glances at* ERIC.

HAROLD A hundred metres, feels like a marathon…

SAM Only think about two things: the gun and the tape. When you hear the one, just run like hell till you break the other.

STARTER Get set.

A pause.

HAROLD Where's that bloody gun!

The gun is fired and they run.

The scoreboard says ten, twenty – they're all together...

Thirty, **ABRAHAMS** *has a lead.*

Forty...a little further. By fifty, he's got a clear lead...

Sixty, seventy, eighty – **ABRAHAMS** *holding it.*

Ninety... And a hundred!

breaks tape

HAROLD ~~*jumps off the treadmill,*~~ *out of breath, the others do the same. There's no noise, no reaction. He stands, in focus – on his own, catching his breath, looking up.*

Tableau

A pause. Everyone still. **HAROLD**'s *moment of uncertainty...what's going on?*

SAM Harold? ~~Has~~ *Did he done it?*

SYBIL *enters, chased by a* **STAGEHAND**.

STAGEHAND ~~Miss Evers! Mrs Abrahams just rang Miss. The~~ Daily Express have been on from Paris. Mr Harold...

TRINITY *and* **CAIUS** *enter.*

CAIUS Well?

TRINITY *gives* **CAIUS** *the newspaper.*

TRINITY Just as I expected.

CAIUS Ah.

The stage shifts – the scenes drifting out as we move to **SAM**'s *room. He's standing in the light from the window, anxious. The sound in the distance of a French announcement, but it's so tinny and indistinct.*

A moment, then the sound of the national anthem begins and the Union Flag is raised. **SAM** *cannot believe it!*

SAM Yes!

He's jubilant. Gets his straw hat and punches his fist through it.

As he does, sudden, huge applause. **ABRAHAMS** *is mobbed.* **SAM** *pours two drinks, and the* **CROWD** *disperses – it's that night.*

SR Truck at back

SAM *gives a drink to* **HAROLD,** *who now clutches his gold medal.*

You've always seen yourself as a ruthless swine, haven't you? Heart of stone. Like me. Actually you're soft as me pocket. You care about the things that matter. If you didn't, I wouldn't have come within a mile of you.

You know, what you've won out there, today? For us.

You and old Sam Mussabini. I've waited. Waited thirty bloody years for this. Walker. No. Applegarth? Phhhh. Thirty years.

Abrahams.

He holds the medal.

HAROLD Yes! Yes!

SAM Harold this means the world to me, you know?

It's ours. For keeps.

It's out of your system now. Done. Forget it.

Just get back to that girl of yours and start some bloody living.

HAROLD *takes his drink and holds it up.*

HAROLD To Sam Mussabini!

The greatest trainer in the world.

SAM Coach.

HAROLD The greatest coach in the world!

SAM stands and clinks glasses. They look at each other,
SAM wanders home.

ERIC enters. It's the next day – the four hundred metres
is set up around ERIC. HAROLD, AUBREY and ANDY
find a place to watch, the PRINCE shaking hands, then
sitting down. The other competitors getting ready. ERIC
goes and shakes their hands.

ERIC All the best.

Have a good race.

Don't expect I'll see you till after.

Mr Scholz. Have a good race.

SCHOLZ hands him a note and exits. ERIC turns and
finds himself facing...

Jennie!

JENNIE Eric, we've read the papers, then Sandy called me.

ERIC And you came.

JENNIE To see you run Eric. We're proud. However you do.
We're all *proud*. You didn't compromise.

He reaches for her and they hug.

TAYLOR This guy Liddell.

COACH He's a flyer. Just wait. After three hundred metres, rigor
mortis'll set in. You'll pull him in on a rope.

STARTER Ready gentlemen!

JENNIE joins SANDY and FLORENCE in the seats. ERIC
goes back to his place.

On your marks.

ERIC *opens* SCHOLZ'*s note.*

SCHOLZ In the old book it says "He that honours me, I will honour. Good luck. Jackson Scholz".

STARTER Set.

Then...

Go!

The gun. ERIC *starts running. But on his own. The others just stand upright.*

The scoreboard marking up the four hundred metres.

A feat of endurance – he's running and running. Further and harder than ever before.

Then his head goes back – the lighting changes – something from the heavens. A hint of God.

The clapperboard hits three hundred-and-sixty; three hundred-and-seventy; three hundred-and-eighty; three hundred-and-ninety. On four hundred, he crosses the line – applause and cheers.

HAROLD *goes to him first – supports him.*

HAROLD You did it Eric! You did it! Exit CB

They embrace. The others gather, now speaking to the audience.

AUBREY Abrahams and Liddell.

ANDY The toast of the nation.

SAM Carried from the train to the car, waving through the streets of London, all of them.

SYBIL Not quite all. I was there, at the station, as I promised. We kissed...he asked me to marry him.

SANDY Eric got his degree, married Florence, and then China. The mission.

JENNIE As he always said he would.

SAM Harold Abrahams became the voice of athletics. The foremost authority.

FLORENCE With the war the children and I came home. But Eric stayed in China, imprisoned, he cared for anyone that needed him. Eventually, he was offered a place out of there...

He gave it to someone else...

He stayed. And died. In the final year of the war.

SANDY In 1996 a Scottish engineer tracked down the place where Eric died, and a headstone was built. An inscription on the front.

AUBREY Harold died in 1978.

ANDY In Hertfordshire. A grave for them both. Sybil Abrahams, Harold Abrahams...

FLORENCE It was the life that mattered.

SYBIL The race they ran.

ERIC Harold was always determined. There's no doubt. When it came down to it.

He was faster.

HAROLD Yes. I was faster.

But Eric was better.

SAM "They shall mount up, with wings as eagles, they shall run, and not be weary".

ABRAHAMS *and* LIDDELL *stand, together...*

The CROWD *sing "JERUSALEM".*

CROWD

BRING ME MY BOW OF BURNING GOLD!

BRING ME MY ARROWS OF DESIRE!
BRING ME MY SPEAR: O CLOUDS UNFOLD!
BRING ME MY CHARIOTS OF FIRE!
I WILL NOT CEASE FROM MENTAL FIGHT;
NOR SHALL MY SWORD SLEEP IN MY HAND
TILL WE HAVE BUILT JERUSALEM
IN ENGLAND'S GREEN AND PLEASANT LAND.

*As the scene fades we focus on a single runner –
contemporary – 2012.*

Epilogue

And now all of them running together. This time celebratory.

Like the beginning, but now fuller, more jubilant.

Everything builds.

Then with a smash!

Blackout.

End

PROPS/LIGHTING/SOUND EFFECTS

ACT I

PROPS

Couple of bags, pair of running shoes attached by the laces (p2)
Bags (p2)
Three bags, books, golf clubs and two tennis racquets (p2)
Bags and books, gowns, hats (p4)
A letter (p5)
Book (p6)
Drinks (p6)
Drink (p7)
Cards (p10)
Poster of Sybil (p10)
Clipboard (p11)
Banners (p12)
Line on the ground using two of the students' hats (p13)
Bottle of champagne (p14)
Bunting (p17)
Bagpipes (p20)
Pistol (p20)
Tables, flowers, bunting (p21)
Silver cup (p21)
Tape (p23)
Bible (p27)
A large sign, which makes it clear – we're at the Scottish
Athletic Association games: Scotland V France – 2nd June 1923
(p30)
Cigarette (p32)
Pistol (p32)
A full D'Oyly Carte production of this scene from The Mikado
enters. Costumes, lights, this is a professional thing (p38)
Opera glasses (p38)
Champagne (p40)
Cocktails (p41)
Menu (p41)
Dishes (p44)
Bike (p44)
Newspaper (p46)

A larger flipping score board – like an old cricket scoreboard counts the metres (p48)
A projector is wheeled on (p51)
Hurdle (p54)
Champagne bottle and two glasses (p55)
A paper (p57)
Drinks (p57)
A piece of paper (p62)

COSTUME

Abrahams – suit and hat (p2)
Reg – scarred, with a bandage across his head, and missing an arm (p4)
Jim – blind, wearing his medals (p4)
Andy – posh suit. Immaculate (p6)
Aubrey – evening suit (p6)
Abrahams – suit (p7)
Abrahams – overcoat (p11)
Aubrey – scarf (p12)
Andy – coat (p14)
Alastair and Colin – shorts and caps (p17)
Eric – tweed suit (p18)
Crowd – some in dancing clothes, others in kilts, running kit (p21)
Sam – straw hat and a moustache (p30)
Harold – evening gear (p40)
Sybil – coat (p40)
Eric – running kit (p44)
Sybil – a coat and hat (p46)
Paddock – running gear (p52)
Ten runners dressed as Harold (p53)
Sybil – a glorious summer dress (p54)
Andy – he takes off his robe – he's wearing his running gear (p56)
Harold – evening dress (p57)

LIGHTING

Sam switches a switch and the room changes to flickering projector light (p52)

Sam switches on the light (p53)
Fade on the scene (p63)
House light – and the Olympic logo for the first time. White on black (p63)

SOUND/EFFECTS

Prologue - Swirling and smoke (p1)
Sound of steam, smoke (p2)
Sound of ringing Cambridge bells (p4)
Knock on the door (p6)
Knock on the door (p6)
The bell sounds twelve times (p15)
Dong! Dong! (p15)
Dong! Dong! (p15)
Dong! Dong! (p15)
Dong! Dong! (p15)
Dong! Dong! (p15)
Dong! (p15)
Champagne is popped (p16)
Bagpipes from off (p19)
Fires the pistol (p21)
Sandy starts playing (bagpipes) (p21)
Sounds the pistol (p23)
A church bell – maybe a hymn in the distance (p23)
A football smashes through the window (p25)
The sound of a hymn being sung (p27)
A crack of thunder (p30)
A bell rings (p32)
Pistol fires (p33)
Swirl of train smoke and city air (p46)
A roar from the crowd (p47)
Gun is fired (p48)
A huge boom (p63)
The Olympic logo for the first time. White on black (p63)

ACT II

PROPS

Banners (p64)
Luggage (p64)
Trolley and a footman both stacked with luggage (p65)
Suitcase (p65)
Luggage (p66)
A banner drops "La VIII Olympiade – Bienvenue á tous – Citius Altius Fortius" (p71)
Megaphone (p72)
Gun (p73)
Chair (p79)
Pulpit (p90)
Jacket and kit (p91)
Note (p91)
Charm (p92)
Clapperboard (p93)
Two drinks (p95)
Gold medal (p95)
Note (p97)
Gun (p98)
Costume
Lord Birkenhead – a cigar and slicked black hair (p65)
Lord Birkenhead – black tie (p78)
Sam – straw hat (p95)

LIGHTING

Flash-bulbs (p64)
Flash-bulbs (p66)
Light from the window (p94)
The lighting changes – something from the heavens. A hint of god (p97)
Blackout (p100)

SOUND/EFFECTS

The ship sounds its siren (p68)
Someone plays the run up of Gilbert and Sullivan (p68)

The siren sounds (p71)
The sound of a foghorn (p71)
The French national anthem (p71)
Fires it (p73)
The gun is fired (p94)
The sound in the distance of a French announcement, but it's so tinny and indistinct (p94)
The national anthem begins and the Union Flag is raised (p95)
The gun (p97)

THIS
IS
NOT
THE
END

Visit samuelfrench.co.uk and discover the best theatre bookshop on the internet

A vast range of plays
Acting and theatre books
Gifts

samuelfrench.co.uk

samuelfrenchltd

samuel french uk

Lightning Source UK Ltd.
Milton Keynes UK
UKHW021019100121
376731UK00005B/139